GREGORY OF ZIMBABWE

Gregory of Zimbabwe

A True Story of
Overcoming Child Abuse
and the
Scandal of Diplomatic Immunity

LEONARD T. GRIES, PH.D.

Fithian Press
SANTA BARBARA • 1993

Design and typography by Jim Cook

Published by Fithian Press
Post Office Box 1525
Santa Barbara, California 93102

LIBRARY OF CONGRESS CATALOGING IN PUBLICATION DATA
Gries, Leonard T., Ph.D.
Gregory of Zimbabwe: a true story of overcoming child abuse and
the scandal of diplomatic immunity / Leonard T. Gries.
p. cm.
ISBN 1-56474-054-4
1. Diplomatic privileges and immunities—United States.
2. Diplomatic and consular service, Zimbabwean—United States.
3. Zimbabweans—Legal status, laws, etc.—New York (N.Y.)
4. Custody of children—New York (N.Y.)
5. Foster home care—Law and legislation—New York (N.Y.)
6. Child abuse—Law and legislation—New York (N.Y.)
7. Dipomats—New York (N.Y.)—Family relationships.
I. Title
JX1671.G 1993
345.747'1025554—dc20
[347.4710525554 93-12552
CIP

To Gregory, and all the abused children that I have come to know: thank you for keeping the warm glow of compassion alive in me, and for teaching the ultimate meaning of courage.

•

To the talented and caring professionals in the child welfare system, the caseworkers, the clinicians, the administrators, and legal personnel: your work, often unrecognized or not appreciated, is among the noblest of endeavors to which one's life can be dedicated.

•

To my parents, Nathan and Lillian, thank you for instilling in me the love of family. To my wife, Susanne, and sons, Jimmy, Adam, and Matthew: thank you for strengthening that feeling of family love and for encouraging me in my work of extending that message to my clients.

Contents

Acknowledgments

SPECIAL THANKS go to several people whose assistance in the preparation of this book is greatly appreciated. The efforts and suggestions of my friend and neighbor, Ms. Andrée Weitz, who proofread the original manuscript, were most helpful. Much gratitude is also felt for my secretary, Ms. Sylvia Norman, whose dedication and skills in typing the original manuscript and revisions mirror the general excellence found in her everyday performance through the years that she has been associated with the Mental Health Services Department of St. Christopher-Ottilie. Thanks also to Dan Rutberg, and Anne Valentine of his staff, for their able and enthusiastic assistance with computer details and printing.

Finally, I am most grateful to my many colleagues and friends at St. Christopher-Ottilie, whose genuine interest, support, and encouragement helped to sustain my drive to complete this work. Heading this list, of course, is Bob McMahon, executive director; Tom Ring, assistant executive director; Gary Kipling, assistant executive director; and Joe Carrieri, attorney. Working so closely with them, with foster care directors Zeyda Fernandez and Yara Fernandez Aldana, and with caseworker Stephanie Rothstein on the case of Gregory was truly one of the most rewarding experiences of my career.

Introduction

W HEN I WAS a child and my mother told my brother and me a bedtime story, I would invariably ask if it was a true story. Stories are sources of much fun and excitement for kids, but true stories offer something extra special. From the time we are old enough to understand, the true story is a vehicle for assisting us in the universal human quest for knowledge. In our never-ending investigation of the various aspects of our existence, we persist in pursuit of a goal that we never actually achieve: absolute truth. Oh, we often delude ourselves into believing that we have attained the level of full and absolute truth in a given area. However, even in the natural sciences, just when we think we've reached the final piece of a scientific puzzle, new pieces always seem to emerge.

Our knowledge about a subject only approximates the ever-elusive absolute truth. Truth is a relative, rather than an absolute, concept. It reflects all that is objectively known about a particular subject, relative to what was known a year ago, and relative to what will be known a year from now. It is relative also because the investigator, in his search for truth, automatically factors in his or her own perceptions and interpretations about what is being seen or heard or felt. One person's truth is, therefore, never quite identical to his neighbor's version.

The following is based on a true story. Only the names of the central character and his immediate family have been changed to protect their privacy. With the exception of the first three chapters, it is a story about actual events that occurred between November

1987 and March 1988; the first three chapters are a dramatization of events reported by others. It reflects my personal and professional version of the truth as it pertains to one particular scourge of human existence found throughout "civilized society" during the latter part of the twentieth century: child abuse. It is told with the consent of the family.

This is a story of child abuse as seen through the eyes of a psychologist intimately involved in a case that received considerable publicity throughout the United States and Africa. In consideration of my earlier comments, the story approximates the truth about child abuse from the perspective of an observer somewhat removed from the central abusive act. The truth according to the child victim, the alleged abuser, or other family members would probably be at odds with my version. Child abuse has a way of sufficiently upsetting all participants and observers to the extent that heightened emotions obfuscate total objectivity. Although there was much physical and testimonial evidence for the acts of abuse described herein, there was never an opportunity to legally prove or disprove the allegations in an American court of law. Any reference to such abusive acts must, therefore, implicitly include the qualifier "alleged."

More than simply looking at what child abuse is and how it manifests itself, this work attempts to help the reader focus on reactions to child abuse. It is only through knowing and understanding the emotional and behavioral sequelae of abuse that we can develop scientific, social, and personal strategies for eliminating it as a blot on humanity. Once child abuse in the home occurs, reactions occur at multiple levels. The child victim reacts psychologically and behaviorally. The child's siblings react. His non-abusing parent reacts. Beyond the immediate family, society reacts in the person of child-protective governmental and private agencies, as well as the family courts. Friends and classmates of the child react, as do adult neighbors or strangers who happen to hear about it. In many instances, surrogate or foster parents are called in and they, too, have reactions to the abuse. In the story to be presented here, the sphere of reaction extends much further to include the media, the public at large, all three branches of the United States government and the government of Zimbabwe.

Reactions to child abuse range from horror to anger and need for vengeance to denial. Each of these emotions is commonplace in the home where abuse has taken place. Similar reactions may occur in the people ostensibly charged with preventing further abuse from occurring. The caseworker may empathetically feel as horrified as her child client. The foster parent may feel extremely angry and vengeful on the child's behalf. The governmental child-protective agency official or the family court judge may discount or even deny the occurrence of alleged acts of abuse. Participants may overreact or underreact. It's quite difficult to achieve just the right degree of objective balance to one's emotional response to child abuse. The health and welfare of the child should take precedence over any and all considerations. When those in the child protection system and/or within government allow their own emotional reactions to come into play, then this principle of prioritizing the child's welfare is likely to be violated. When agenda and priorities other than the child's welfare assume a position of primary importance, the system set up by society to protect its young from their own misguided or disturbed parents will fail.

This, then, is a true story, told with the intention of illustrating how our society works effectively and ineffectively at the task of protecting its young. The working assumption is that the more each of us learns about the facts and myths of child abuse, the closer we as a society will get to that elusive, unobtainable goal: the absolute truth. This is the best approach I know that can bring us closer to the day when a story such as this one could be only a nightmarish fairy tale.

1. "Don't Tell Me
How to Raise My Child"

P.S. 178 is a public elementary school situated in Jamaica Estates, a section of Queens, New York, populated primarily by middle- to upper-middle-class families. In a public school system repeatedly under attack for its deteriorating standards, P.S. 178 is one school that has enjoyed a fine reputation. Its students have included the children of successful businessmen, local politicians, and professionals. During the fall of 1987, two of its students were Gregory and Kim Tanaka of Zimbabwe, Africa. Gregory (nine years old), Kim (seven), and their sister Cynthia (three) are the children of Philip and Leila Tanaka. The family came to New York from Harare, Zimbabwe, in September 1986 when Mr. Tanaka received an assignment with the Zimbabwean mission to the United Nations. Although initially enrolled in a Catholic parochial school in Manhattan, Gregory and Kim were transferred to P.S. 178 in the spring of 1987 when the family moved into a one-family home on Midland Parkway, not far from the school.

As Thanksgiving 1987 approached, the Tanakas received a call from the school guidance counselor requesting a meeting with both parents concerning Gregory. Gregory's school performance and behavior had been a source of concern for school officials throughout his school career, including the time that he had attended a parochial school in Zimbabwe. He had consistently performed below grade level and was distant from peers and teachers alike. While he was at P.S. 178, it was reported that Gregory did not respond appropriately to authority, and was instead withdrawn and hostile. The school had been prepared to enroll him in a special Resource Room Program, where individual attention would be available. The Tanakas were prepared for still another discouraging conference concerning Gregory's school problems as they entered the guidance counselor's office. What transpired instead was a brief, unexpected confrontation that would dramatically alter their lives and Gregory's.

Rather than speak about Gregory's school performance, the guidance counselor alluded to some scars on Gregory's wrists that had been noticed by his teacher. Gregory had been closed-mouthed when asked about the scars, thus raising suspicions that foul play of some kind was involved. One possible explanation that needed to be ruled out was that the scars may have resulted from his being physically abused. School officials are legally mandated to investigate and report to appropriate authorities any suspected incident of child abuse.

November 1987 was a time of considerable alarm and chagrin concerning the welfare of children in New York City and throughout the United States. Reports of physical and sexual abuse of children were reaching epidemic proportions, resulting in a doubling of referrals for foster-care placement between 1986 and 1987. Explanations for this dramatic rise included the significant rise in drug use (particularly crack cocaine), the AIDS crisis, the worsening low-income housing shortage in most urban areas, and the decreasing number of young adults receiving adequate educational and vocational preparation for life. The dissolution of the American family was an equally significant co-factor that contributed to the overall problem. Such reasoning implied a solution. If families could remain intact, if parents could receive sufficient education to ensure adequate income, and if decent housing were affordable and the family's standard of living could be maintained, then perhaps the incidence of child abuse would be substantially reduced.

Public opinion and interest in this issue received a remarkable jolt on November 3, 1987, when the Lisa Steinberg tragedy came to light. Lisa was the adopted daughter of an attorney and a writer of children's books. The well-to-do couple lived in a Greenwich

Village brownstone once occupied by Mark Twain. Lisa had died of wounds received from chronic beatings, allegedly at the hands of her father. There had been prior indications of family strife and possible abuse in the home. Neighbors had reported hearing piercing screams from the apartment; a toll booth patrolman had noted Lisa's downtrodden condition. Yet, authorities had not come up with sufficient evidence to remove Lisa and her younger brother from the apartment. The responsible city child welfare agency could not, and had not, protected Lisa, despite the warning signs. The public was enraged, astonished, frightened, and guilt-ridden about the event. How could such brutal beatings occur? How could this have involved educated professionals with such comfortable living conditions? Could it happen just as easily in the homes of middle-class friends and neighbors? Why hadn't Lisa Steinberg been protected?

Now, three weeks after Lisa Steinberg's death, responsible adults were vigilant. No similar tragedy should be allowed to happen. With such universal concern in the air, people were not as reluctant to speak out in defense of defenseless children. When the P.S. 178 guidance counselor asked the Tanakas about Gregory's scars, there was perhaps less concern about embarrassment and making false accusations than in the past. To the guidance counselor's astonishment, Mr. Tanaka readily admitted that he was the cause of his son's scars. They resulted, he said, from spankings that he gave to Gregory for punitive reasons. Mr. Tanaka steadfastly believed in the correctness of his actions. Corporal punishment was his method of choice for eliminating Gregory's defiant and sometimes hostile behavior at school. As her husband spoke, Mrs. Tanaka sat quietly next to him, making no remark or gesture that would indicate her agreement or disagreement with what he was saying.

Undaunted, the guidance counselor replied, "This type of child-rearing practice is not allowed in this country. It must stop. If it continues, I will have no choice but to notify the city's child-protective agency [Special Services for Children]."

Although Mr. Tanaka showed no visible reaction to the guidance counselor's warning, he was seething inside as he and his wife began their drive home.

"How dare anyone try to tell me how I should handle my child," he muttered to his wife. "I am a member of the diplomatic corps of my country. No one, except for my comrades at the embassy, am I to listen to. This is an affront to me, to my president, and to the Republic of Zimbabwe."

Mrs. Tanaka, in hope of placating her husband with some soothing music, turned on the car radio. The news was reporting on the continuing Lisa Steinberg case. Philip Tanaka abruptly turned off the radio and glared.

The following weekend, in one of the first celebrations of the 1987 Christmas season, a reception was held at the Zimbabwean mission to the United Nations. It was a semi-formal affair, with all mission staff and their spouses present. The Zimbabwean ambassador and his wife hosted the party, which included invited guests primarily from the missions of other third-world countries. Philip and Leila Tanaka arrived exactly on time and promptly began to mingle with other Zimbabwean couples. Lighthearted discussions could not fully hide the tension the Tanakas felt. Although Mr. Tanaka had been posted at the U.N. mission for fifteen months, he still didn't feel as if he fully belonged. Was it his own perception, or was it a fact that he was excluded from some of the staff meetings where the more urgent matters were discussed? Socially, too, the Tanakas felt a subtle distancing by other couples. Standing in the center of the reception area with several other couples, Mrs. Tanaka excused herself to go to the ladies' room to freshen up. Simultaneously, Mr. Tanaka went off to get drinks. As both walked deliberately to their destinations, they suddenly heard chuckles and laughter from the people they had just left. Was the laughter about them?

Philip Tanaka was born in what was then British-ruled Rhodesia in 1950. Leila, six years his junior, was also born and raised in Rhodesia. The couple met and married shortly thereafter, in 1978. In deference to tribal custom, the groom was required first to pay the *tabola* (bride-wealth or dowry). The newlyweds quickly became respected members of a nearby United Methodist congregation. It was a fulfilling and exciting time. Gregory, their first child, was born later the same year. Political change was in the air as well, and Philip was thrilled to be in on the ground floor of the movement for independence. Within months of Gregory's birth, the independent Republic of Zimbabwe was proclaimed. Philip eagerly became involved with the new government. Eventually, he joined the Ministry of Foreign Affairs, but, for whatever reasons, did not receive his first foreign posting until the U.N. assignment in September 1986.

This was the opportunity the Tanakas had been patiently awaiting since they married. They had waited too long for anything to go wrong and spoil things. It was difficult to fathom just how far each had come—from their rural, tribal beginnings to the international "fast lane" of New York City. With the excited anticipation came tension and apprehension; nothing must go wrong! Leila's life and opportunities for future growth were defined by her husband's political fortunes. Her primary job was to support her husband's efforts so as to further his career. If disagreements or reservations existed, she was careful to disguise any such concerns. She fulfilled her role as dutiful lieutenant, asking no questions and taking no independent stances about anything. She knew her place; women's lib had not yet arrived in Zimbabwe, nor had it arrived within the Tanaka household. She knew better than to challenge her husband on any issue, even within the traditionally female domain of child-rearing.

2. Terror in the Night

F OR NINE-YEAR-OLD Gregory Tanaka, school had never been fun. For as long as he could remember, it had always been a struggle, often with other children, but most consistently with teachers. Two factors weighed heavily upon him. It seemed that he just never could measure up academically to the expectations that others had of him. The more he experienced disappointment, the less he subsequently tried. By the time he entered the fourth grade, his tested reading level placed him in the 13th percentile for his age group. He was underachieving. The second factor concerned a clash of personalities between Gregory and authority figures. Gregory regularly opposed the instructions and regulations that teachers attempted to impose on him. In his school reports he was described as disobedient and defiant. There was an almost daily battle that Gregory waged at school. It was a battle for control; a battle for autonomy.

Gregory's academic and behavioral difficulties at school served to exacerbate his precarious social position among his peers. His tiny physical stature, along with his foreign background, helped alienate him from his classmates. Gregory, in fact, didn't seem that interested in interacting with other children. Most of his energies seemed to focus on his frequent battles with authority and on other concerns remote from the classroom—concerns about a troubled home life. Gregory seemed a brazen, troubled, underachieving, and socially isolated youngster.

On Wednesday, December 9, Gregory's class was engaged in a routine assignment when his teacher looked up from her desk and noticed that Gregory's attention was not on his work. Daydreaming was not uncommon for Gregory; he always seemed to have more important things on his mind. The teacher furtively approached the child's desk without his being aware. Just as she moved to within a foot of his desk, she yelled, "Gregory, what are you doing?"

The startled boy dropped what he had been holding and examining. It was a twenty-dollar bill. A cross examination by the teacher failed to produce a clear picture of how Gregory came to have the bill. He claimed to have been given the bill to hold by another child, but this could not be substantiated. The teacher suspected theft. Gregory had been implicated during several incidents earlier in the year. After class, she telephoned Mrs. Tanaka and informed her about what had transpired. Mrs. Tanaka immediately called her husband at the Zimbabwean mission. As he was in conference, he was forced to suppress the intense feelings of exasperation and anger that he was experiencing inside. His thoughts drifted to his troublesome son, a constant thorn in his side and an ever-present potential embarrassment for the family. Philip knew what he had to do when he arrived home later in the evening.

When Gregory arrived home from school, he knew he was in for an ordeal. He had been down this road numerous times in the past. With his sisters gawking with excited anticipation, his mother verbally lashed out at Gregory. Little Kim and Cynthia were somewhat frightened, but relieved that, once again, their brother would be the one to receive the parental wrath about to be unleashed. Gregory was clearly the "bad guy" of the family. Leila sent her son to his room as she invoked her husband's name. "Your father will take care of this when he gets home."

Waiting for his father was the worst time for Gregory. He knew what was coming. The pattern had been established when the family still lived in Zimbabwe. Memories of life seven thousand miles away flashed across his consciousness. Sure, he always seemed to be getting into trouble because of one misdeed or another, which invariably occurred away from home. Father was the disciplinarian. Following each transgression was sure to be some form of punishment. Punishments had become more intensely physical since the Tanakas had come to New York. As far back as Gregory could remember, however, the pattern of disappointing and angering father, leading to parental admonition and ultimately to some form of corporal punishment, was a familiar one. Gregory couldn't help but have the conviction that he was the "bad seed" of the family, although he seldom if ever acknowledged this outwardly.

The front door opened and slammed shut. The muffled voices of Mr. Tanaka and his wife could be heard by Gregory as he lay on his bed. Footsteps, getting louder with each step toward the bedroom door, generated an immediate hastening of his thumping heart. Gregory, head down on his pillow, took a deep breath as the door to his room opened and his father entered like an executioner.

In a deep monotone, devoid of emotion, Philip spoke: "Come with me."

Gregory's heart raced as he envisioned a repetition of a ritual that was becoming more and more commonplace. When he hesitated, his father firmly grabbed his arm. Gregory immediately pulled back in a futile attempt to stay on his bed. He repeated the word "No" over and over, more loudly each time. Finally, Philip half-dragged his son from the bedroom into the hallway and down the stairs to the large, unfinished basement. As they descended, Philip asked his wife to come along with the two girls. Reaching the basement, Philip immediately ripped off most of Gregory's clothing and bound his arms together with rope. Philip hoisted his half-naked son into the air, fastening the end of one rope around a pipe that ran along the ceiling. As Gregory hung suspended four or five feet above the floor, he braced himself both physically and psychologically for what was to come. He tensed just about every muscle in his body and became motionless. He no longer attempted to communicate with his incensed father or with his seemingly unsympathetic mother and sisters, who dutifully stood near the foot of the stairs. Gregory could only visualize his father preparing to mete out the first of twenty lashes with an electrical cord. The first lash struck with a resounding thump as mother and sisters cringed in the background. Gregory felt a piercing bolt of pain along his upper back. When Philip glanced back at his wife and daughters, they instantaneously began to yell at Gregory derisively.

"Serves you right! Bad Gregory! Again! Hit him harder!"

It is difficult to say which hurt Gregory more, the physical pain inflicted by his father or the emotional pain inflicted by the rest of his family. Gregory was able to do something about the physical pain. He blocked it out by employing a psychological defense known as dissociation. His eyes fluttered rapidly, and then rolled upward so that only the whites showed. It was as if part of Gregory—the conscious, human part—left his body, escaping awareness of the damage being done. With each blow the family continued to jeer, while Gregory became more and more oblivious. Finally, the twentieth blow was administered; Gregory's entire body was marked and bloodied, with bits of flesh missing at points where the cord had struck the hardest. The rope that kept Gregory suspended in the air was abruptly released by his father, causing the boy to come crashing head-first to the cement floor. Blood seeped from the resulting wound to his forehead. As Gregory was led away, he stared disdainfully but silently at his sisters. This particular ordeal was over.

"Maybe now he has learned his lesson," Philip thought as he returned to the living room.

Unbeknownst to Philip, Gregory was learning many lessons, none of which resembled the one intended by his father. He had learned to be terrified of his father, and, despite fantasies of revenge, he wanted nothing more than to leave his father forever. He had learned that there was virtually no one in the world to whom he could turn for help or support—not even his mother. He felt so terribly alone and helpless. Gregory had also learned to despise himself, his weaknesses, his helplessness, and his sense of total inadequacy. He yearned to be powerful and in control, like his father. Unfortunately, the only opportunity to feel that way came at school or in other settings where he purposefully defied authority. The more he was subjugated and made to feel worthless at home, the more he pursued his quest to be autonomous and in control away from home.

As he lay in bed that night, Gregory vowed that he had had enough of this life of torture and terror. But he was so tiny and insignificant. What could he possibly do to save himself? Who would believe him? Once before, several months earlier, following a similar beating, Gregory called 911 in desperation. When the police arrived, his mother refuted the child's allegations to their satisfaction. Gregory was then beaten again after his mother informed Philip of the call to the police.

3. A Cry for Help

AFTER REMAINING at home on Thursday, Gregory returned to school on Friday, December 11. He went right to his seat and sat quietly, much more subdued than usual. His teacher, who did not notice him at first, looked in his direction as she took attendance. She was aghast at what she saw. Gregory's forehead was mutilated, a large patch of skin missing over his left eye. He made no reply when asked what had happened, and was immediately sent to the nurse's office. The school guidance counselor and principal were called in, and they, too, looked on in horror as Gregory was examined.

Even more horrifying than the forehead wound were numerous scars that crisscrossed his back. Some of the scars appeared to be from old wounds, whereas others appeared to be of more recent origin. Although hesitant at first, Gregory eventually began to divulge the true story behind his wounds and scars. He described how his father methodically whipped him over and over again while Gregory was suspended in mid-air.

As he spoke, his voice, almost inaudible at first, betrayed a suppressed rage. He was careful to include the fact that his mother and sisters seemed to approve of, if not enjoy witnessing, the brutality that his father heaped on him. Gregory was encouraged by the school officials to reveal the entire story of what had happened to him at home. Although still terribly frightened and despondent, there was the faintest glimmer of hope in Gregory's eyes. Finally, at long last, someone was listening to his long-held secret. Was it possible that help would be forthcoming?

A call was made to the New York City Special Services for Children (SSC). School officials were unanimous in their conviction that the abuse must be reported and that protective measures must be taken to ensure the safety of Gregory and his two sisters. No one wanted another Lisa Steinberg!

Kim, who also attended P.S. 178, was escorted from her classroom to the principal's office, where Gregory, the school principal, and the guidance counselor were waiting. The two children's eyes met, and Kim seemed to know exactly what was going on without even asking a question. When the SSC worker arrived, Gregory willingly repeated his story.

"Don't send me back to my father," he cried. "I never want to see him or my mother again!"

Kim was questioned separately. Her account confirmed the story given by her brother, acknowledging that Gregory had been hit or whipped on numerous occasions. She could recall only one incident in which she had received comparable physical punishment. Nevertheless, Kim offered no resistance to going with her brother and the caseworker to an unknown destination. Despite reports that she had jeered while Gregory was being beaten, it was obvious that Kim was quite attached to her brother and very much wished to remain with him, even if it meant being separated from the rest of the family.

Just prior to leaving the school with the two children, the SSC caseworker placed a call to her office advising her supervisor to arrange for another worker to take the youngest child, Cynthia, into custody. In order to minimize the possibility of a struggle or other incident, a police officer accompanied the second caseworker to the Tanaka home. Mrs. Tanaka appeared at the front door and stood in the doorway as the caseworker introduced herself and explained the purpose of the visit. She was informed of the allegations of child abuse necessitating the temporary placement of all three of her children into protective custody. Her countenance was transformed from puzzlement to anger in a matter of seconds.

"Where did you take my children?" she exclaimed. "You have

no right to do this! Who do you think you are?" She quickly regained her composure as she resolutely declared, "You may not enter my home. Get off my property this instant. This is the home of a diplomat. Get out of here!"

The caseworker and the police officer retreated to the foot of the front steps.

"We get this all the time," she whispered. "Don't worry, we have the right to enter any home where a child's welfare is at stake. Let's do this as quickly as possible."

The officer called to her as she took her first steps back to the door. "Ma'am, we can't go in."

The caseworker interrupted, "Of course we can go in. Let's go before we attract a crowd."

The officer persisted. "We can't go in. The family has diplomatic immunity."

This was the first time that this term was mentioned in this case. It would not be the last. The caseworker and police officer left without another word being spoken. The privacy of the home of a diplomat's staff member remained inviolate.

Back at SSC headquarters, the novelty and sensitivity of the Tanaka case was beginning to sink in. By seizing Gregory and Kim, the city agency may have already been in violation of international convention regarding diplomatic immunity.

"This could be a real hot potato," uttered one administrator. "Let's not do anything in haste. Don't even arrange for the routine physical examination yet."

5. The Legal Tug-of-War Begins

GREGORY AND KIM were placed in the temporary custody of the Special Services for Children program of the City of New York Human Resources Administration. Pending a dispositional hearing in family court, they were sent to live in the home of a black family in Freeport on Long Island. The family had been approved to serve in a foster-care capacity, and was registered with St. Christopher-Ottilie Services for Children and Families, a private, voluntary child care agency. Within hours, Gregory and Kim found themselves among loving strangers with open arms. Gregory felt safe for the first time in recent memory.

At the U.S. mission to the U.N., several officials of the U.S. Department of State are assigned the responsibility of playing host to the scores of foreign dignitaries who visit or work at the United Nations. They serve as links between dignitaries and city, state, and federal governments.

On the morning of December 12, the calls from the Zimbabwean mission to the United Nations began. Zimbabwean officials demanded the immediate return of Gregory and Kim. They were irate at the thought that a local government agency could "kidnap" the children of a foreign dignitary at whim. The State Department official listened patiently as the Zimbabwean representative let off some steam on the phone. He assured the representative that he would look into the matter and rectify the problem in as brief a time as possible. He then placed a call to SSC, where an

28

SSC supervisor detailed the nature of the alleged physical abuse. The SSC supervisor informed the State Department official that there was incontrovertible physical evidence that Gregory had been whipped forcefully and repeatedly, causing him to sustain pronounced wounds and scars on his back, arms, legs, and forehead. This was not a marginal or questionable case of abuse; it was blatant.

Although Kim was frightened, too, it was Gregory who was terrified of being returned to his parents. No scars were found on Kim, only on Gregory. While Kim showed signs of wanting to return to her family even though she wanted to remain with her brother, Gregory was emphatic in his desire to stay away from his family and away from the Zimbabwean government officials. He stated his desire to remain with his foster family—to remain in America.

The State Department official, beginning to realize that this was going to be a bit more complicated than he had first imagined, looked further into the allegations of child abuse. He ordered pictures to be taken of Gregory's injuries and requested the report of a physical examination. All supported the finding that substantial physical abuse had occurred. Furthermore, he learned that Philip Tanaka admitted to beating his son as a means of disciplining him. Under the government's authority to expel a diplomat accused of violating the law, the State Department ordered Mr. Tanaka's removal from the United States on December 20. He left the U.S. on December 21. State Department officials were quoted as saying that they had "ample evidence that Tanaka had engaged in systematic and brutal abuse of his children."

On December 21, with Philip Tanaka now out of the country, the State Department official confidently called SSC and, now that it was safe with Mr. Tanaka gone, requested that Gregory and his sister be returned to the Zimbabwean mission.

The SSC supervisor responded, "I'm sorry to put a monkey wrench in this, but the boy still doesn't want to leave, and the girl isn't so sure herself. I think you should speak with the Legal Aid Society on this. They are the children's law guardian, and I understand that they're planning to do something in court."

The State Department official, undaunted but a little flustered, called the Legal Aid Society. He attempted to placate the concerns voiced on the other end, giving reassurances that everything would be okay and that the children would be protected by the Zimbabwean mission officials.

"The bottom line is the children have to go back. I know they're afraid, but tell them they have nothing to worry about."

The Legal Aid attorney hung up the phone thinking, "They just don't understand how horrible all this has been for the kids."

A hearing in Queens family court was set for Tuesday, December 22. Representing the children was a Legal Aid Society attorney, who was appointed as the law guardian to protect their interests. The law guardian and the corporation counsel, representing Special Services for Children of the City of New York, moved that Gregory and Kim should be placed in the foster-care system for a period of eighteen months. This was based on the argument that there should be a finding of abuse or neglect against the children's parents.

Attorneys representing the U.S. State Department argued that the family court had no jurisdiction in this matter, since Mr. Tanaka and his family had diplomatic immunity. The court agreed that it had no jurisdiction to place Gregory or Kim into foster care. The judge ordered that the State Department must be given custody and arrange for the transfer of the children to the Zimbabwean mission to the United Nations. But the judge stayed the release for twenty-four hours so that the law guardian could appeal the ruling.

Within that period of time, Kim grew more and more distressed about being away from her mother and eventually requested that she be returned. Although heartsick over the prospects of being separated from her brother, she very much felt the need to be back with her mother. She did not harbor anything like the intense fear that Gregory experienced, as her brother was the only child regularly subjected to physical beatings. All attention now focused on Gregory.

Back in their temporary foster home on Long Island, Gregory and Kim were prepared for their last evening together under the same roof. There was much bickering and arguing. Gregory was obviously hostile toward Kim. The basis for his anger was his perception that once again he was going to be the one outsider in the family—the family scapegoat. He couldn't forget how Kim had jeered along with her mother while the beatings were meted out by his father. No one came to Gregory's side, even to lend moral support. Now he sensed that Kim was about to desert him, leaving him without any family. They argued and fought until they were both too tired to continue. Kim fell off to a restful sleep for her last night in foster care. Gregory fell asleep, but awoke several hours later. Plagued by dreams of being beaten by his father once again, he screamed in his sleep.

6. Reasons for Staying

THE MORNING OF Wednesday, December 23, found Gregory only hours away from being released into the custody of Zimbabwean officials. The family court judge had given child welfare officials until 4:00 P.M. to provide sufficient justification for keeping him in foster care. An urgent call was placed to the director of the Queens foster care office of St. Christopher-Ottilie, Services for Children and Families.

Zeyda Fernandez, who had emigrated from Cuba after Castro took over, was a seasoned veteran in the field of child welfare. Yet in her decades of experience she had come across few child-abuse cases that had as horrifying an impact on her. She was informed of the need to have immediate psychological evaluations for Gregory and Kim in time for the family court hearing that afternoon.

Zeyda raced down the hall and into my office to fill me in on the details and on the need for emergency evaluations. Prior to that time, I had known nothing about the case. As a psychologist for nineteen years (eight of those years as director of Mental Health Services at St. Christopher-Ottilie), I had been involved in my share of heart-wrenching and sometimes tragic cases. Most gratifying were those seemingly lost causes in which, through psychological intervention, I was able to make a difference. Gregory's plight, as described by Zeyda, clearly fell into this category and presented a clear challenge that was intensified by the imposed time limit. There in my sixth-floor office overlooking the Jamaica terminal of the Long Island Railroad and the new regional Social Security Administration Center, Zeyda Fernandez quickly briefed me on the events of the past twenty-four hours. One pointed question that needed to be addressed was whether Gregory wanted political asylum in the United States.

At approximately 10:30 A.M. there was a knock at my office door. Before I had a chance to respond, Zeyda walked in with Gregory. At this first moment of meeting, little did any of us know or anticipate the drama that lay ahead. Gregory was so quiet, so tiny, so vulnerable. I just couldn't picture this unassuming child being subjected to the torturous treatment that Zeyda had earlier described to me. I had to hear it from him; but seldom does an evaluator just jump into probing questions about a child's past abusive experiences during the early part of an initial interview.

Gregory responded in an impassive manner to innocuous questions about his history, without emotion or change in facial expression. His voice was almost inaudible as he stated his name and age and date of birth. He volunteered that he was born on the anniversary of President Kennedy's assassination. Only minutes after our meeting, Gregory was revealing a macabre association between his being, his identity, and death. This connection was reinforced by an earlier school report that included a statement made by Gregory: "I get respect when I die."

It wasn't long before Gregory described the abuses to which he had been subjected. He told about the allegations of stealing money at school, but insisted that he was merely holding money for a friend. He showed me the scars on his arms and wrists where he had been tied up with an electric cord during the beatings. When asked what wishes he had, he said that he had two: "Stay with my foster mother until I grow up, and that they do the same to my father as he did to me."

Gregory said emphatically that he wanted to have nothing to do with his father, his mother, or any other family member. Gregory unhesitatingly declared that, if forced to live with his family or with the Zimbabwean ambassador, he would run away, but his destination was indeterminate. His fear of living with the Zimbabwean ambassador, or with any Zimbabwean national, emanated from his conviction that others would immediately return him to his father.

Projective psychological tests were administered and supported a picture of a highly defensive, constricted, yet determined youngster. Apparently Gregory successfully defended himself against potential negative reaction to past experiences by shutting off emotion. He was thereby able to preserve a fairly positive view of himself, as exemplified in his human figure drawing. Somehow he maintained an identity that was clearly differentiated from the rest of his family. Of significance was the finding that almost all of Gregory's projective material concerned maternal figures and themes—mothers were depicted as failing to help their children to fulfill their needs. The mood of sadness connected with such maternal failure was predominant within Gregory's projective stories, whereas there was an avoidance of confronting feelings about father figures. It was clear that Gregory was experiencing considerable emotional turmoil surrounding mother-child relationships.

A second significant finding was that Gregory's functioning deteriorated when he was required to face emotionally eliciting projective stimuli. This occurred when he was presented with the most colorful of the ink blots found in the Rorschach test. I stated in my subsequent report, "It may be speculated that Gregory's overall functioning, including his capacity to reason rationally and to act in a safe, responsible fashion, would be compromised in emotionally laden situations."

Gregory's interview and testing were completed by 12:30 P.M. Information on his adjustment during his eleven-day stay at his foster home was then reviewed via a phone conversation with the foster mother. She confided, "Gregory was happy all of the time. . . . He didn't want to leave. . . . He ate and slept okay." She added that Gregory sometimes had complained of headaches. The only time he wasn't calm was when there was mention of his parents.

It was almost 3:00 P.M. by the time the findings and recommendations were fully outlined and organized. Joe Carrieri, attorney for St. Christopher-Ottilie for about fifteen years, called from the family court to get the results. I gave him my professional opinion that forcing Gregory to leave what he considered to be his only island of safety might result in a major depressive episode and/or in his acting out of desperation and placing himself unwittingly in jeopardy. Retention in his foster home was strongly urged, as was psychotherapy. My concluding sentences read: "Finally, Gregory's appropriate assertive response (such as calling authorities for help) must not go unnoticed or unreinforced. To do so would merely teach him despair and hopelessness."

Early in our interview, Gregory had remarked on the differences between life in New York and life in Zimbabwe. For one, there were no subways in Zimbabwe. More important for Gregory, in Zimbabwe children weren't able to call the police for help, as he had done in the fall. It takes courage, often born of desperation, for a child to go outside of his family for help in securing protection from the family. How discouraging it would be for Gregory to have such acts of courage ignored and eventually extinguished.

7. The State Department Roller Coaster

J OE CARRIERI presented my findings to State Department officials as well as to the family court judge. From a legal standpoint, the U.S. government argued that, because diplomatic immunity applied to the entire Tanaka family, the family court had no jurisdiction over any Tanaka family member and, therefore, no jurisdiction to place Gregory in foster care.

The court agreed with this argument, and an order transferring custody of the child to the State Department was signed. Although sympathetic to the points raised by Carrieri about Gregory's fragile psychological condition, the court simply could not ignore the fact that it had no jurisdiction in matters pertaining to individuals covered by diplomatic immunity.

Despite this legal setback, positive inroads were made in convincing State Department officials that special consideration of Gregory's psychological condition was needed. Prior to the judge's ruling, Carrieri approached Igou Allbray, assistant U.S. attorney from the Eastern District of New York and chief of the task force representing the U.S. government. Carrieri explained the results and recommendations of the psychological evaluation. Allbray appeared to be very sympathetic and wished to support the professional recommendations aimed at safeguarding Gregory's emotional well-being.

He listened while Gregory's law guardian from the Legal Aid Society, the corporation counsel representing the City of New

York, and Carrieri gave an impassioned account of what they thought the child needed.

Allbray responded, "I feel that it is quite possible that a 120-day humanitarian leave may be granted Gregory by the Immigration and Naturalization Service. Nobody wants to see this child harmed any more than he already has been."

The attorneys for New York City and St. Christopher-Ottilie were gratified to hear this. It appeared that their efforts of the past few days would pay dividends. They reasoned that 120 days would at least give much-needed time to take whatever subsequent steps were needed to protect Gregory. One course of action would be to pursue the possibility of attaining political asylum for the child. This was the path espoused by the Legal Aid Society.

The sense of accomplishment shared by Gregory's advocates was short-lived. Within twenty-four hours, all talk about a humanitarian leave was dropped. Attention was focused instead on the U.S. government's intention to take physical custody of Gregory as soon as possible. We at St. Christopher-Ottilie asked ourselves, "What about the 120-day leave?"

We never found out how or why that plan had been dropped. We could only draw our own inferences. It was generally concluded that some higher-up at the State Department had probably nixed it. It was our first experience of inconsistency and contradiction among officials of the State Department. It would not be our last.

With the support and sympathy of the State Department in doubt again, efforts in the legal domain were intensified during the week between Christmas and New Year's Day. The Legal Aid Society, under the direction of Lenore Gittis, Esq., appealed the family court's order to the appellate division, requesting that the order transferring custody to the State Department be stayed. When this request was denied, an appeal was made to the Court of Appeals, the highest court of the State of New York. A stay was denied by that court as well.

As New Year's Eve approached, it appeared that all legal avenues for protecting Gregory had been exhausted. The family court, the appellate division, and the state Court of Appeals were unable to rule in Gregory's behalf because none had jurisdiction over the welfare of a child whose relationship to a diplomat cloaked him in the all-encompassing shield of diplomatic immunity.

The State Department, armed with the family court order bestowing upon it Gregory's guardianship and under mounting pressure from Zimbabwe to return the child to members of the Zimbabwean mission to the U.N., was eager to effect an immediate resolution of the whole affair. There were growing concerns that American diplomats and their families abroad were in jeopardy of being kidnapped by adversaries of the U.S. in sympathy with Zimbabwe.

In Harare, Zimbabwe's capital city, a headline in its major newspaper, *The Herald,* on the morning of December 30 read: "Zimbabwe Angry Over Child Seizure." The story described Gregory's father as "very humane and a churchgoer," implying his innocence of committing any acts of child abuse. In the same issue, an editorial speculated:

> Gregory Tanaka may be a simple pawn in a grander game to demean the name of Zimbabwe in the eyes of the international community at the U.N. It can only be hoped that the U.N. itself, whose convention with the U.S. government is being so blatantly trampled upon, will make it very clear to the Reagan Administration that such violations will not be tolerated.

What had started out as a sad case of child abuse and had grown into a jurisdictional issue within the New York state courts now qualified as an international dispute of potentially alarming magnitude. At the State Department's Bureau of African Affairs in Washington, frantic messages were transmitted through diplomatic channels assuring the Robert Mugabe government that Gregory would be returned very shortly, now that the last legal hurdles had been cleared. The U.S. government was intent on placating the young African nation, which had achieved its independence only eight years earlier. Although reputed to have Marxist leanings, Zimbabwe was still counted among several new states that were playing significant roles in the shaping of post-colonial Africa. To antagonize or insult Zimbabwe would be to risk insulting its fledgling neighbors, all of whom were striving for acceptance and full recognition on the world stage. The delays over Gregory's status in the United States were perceived as an affront to Zimbabwe's sovereignty. Such an affront is magnified a hundredfold when it involves a nation in its infancy, striving feverishly to establish its own identify among the nations of the world.

Internally, President Mugabe was on the verge of consolidating political power that had eluded him since becoming prime minister in 1980. Civil strife between Mugabe's Shona ethnic group and the rival Ndebele ethnic group, headed by Joshua Nkomo, had undermined the development of the new nation and threatened the security of the government. Now there was the promise of an end to guerrilla fighting as President Mugabe prepared to incorporate Nkomo's Zimbabwe African People's Union into the government. At the very moment that a new image of unity behind one unquestioned leader was being cast, along came the case of Gregory, which threatened to tarnish the much-desired cloak of respectability for which Mugabe was striving. In Harare, Mugabe issued clear and firm guidelines to his ministers at home and in New York. "Get that boy back here immediately. We cannot tolerate being treated as though we were a second-rate country of no consequence. The world and our people must recognize our position as a sovereign nation."

At the State Department, the pressure to honor the internationally accepted conventions of diplomatic immunity and the political pressure to avoid any further antagonism of third-world nations combined to form a compelling argument in behalf of the immediate transfer of Gregory to his nationals. It remained only for our government to receive some form of reassurance that Gregory would receive any necessary protection from the Zimbabwean government. On December 30, the State Department contacted Janet Fink, a lawyer for the Legal Aid Society, and informed her of what was purported to be an acceptable plan guaranteeing safeguards for Gregory. A Harare law firm retained by the United States prepared a summary of Zimbabwean regulations concerning child welfare. It cited the Department of Social Welfare as the government agency charged with attending to cases of abuse and neglect of children. Reference was made to the Children's Protection and Adoption Act, which provided for the protection of minors and for the punishment of offenders. The report emphasized that "the courts of Zimbabwe can and do take action against their own nationals who commit offenses on foreign soil. This applies particularly in the case of embassy officials. . . ."

State Department officials now believed that Zimbabwe had sufficient institutional and procedural safeguards in place to ensure Gregory's safety upon his return to Zimbabwe. It supported the contention of the Zimbabwean government that it was quite capable of handling matters of child abuse in as professional and enlightened a fashion as might occur in the U.S. The State Department was ready to act without addressing the one remaining issue: the psychological status of Gregory and the risks attached to his immediate transfer.

8. He Must Not Go!

I WAS AT home on the morning of Thursday, December 31, preparing for a restful four-day holiday when the phone rang. It was Joe Carrieri.

He informed me of the State Department's plan, based on the latest reassurances received from Harare, to take custody of Gregory within the next day or two. Joe asked if I would reevaluate Gregory that afternoon to further determine his psychological status, particularly in view of the facts that his departure was now imminent and he would be protected by a child-protection system similar to the one protecting him in New York.

The evaluation was scheduled for 2:00 P.M. at the administrative offices of St. Christopher-Ottilie in Sea Cliff, New York. As I embarked on the ten-minute ride to Sea Cliff, I mulled over what approach to take. After all, I had interviewed Gregory thoroughly and administered all of the basic projective personality tests (Thematic Apperception Test, Rorschach, Sentence Completion Test, Human Figure Drawings and Associations) just eight days earlier. Retesting would provide little if any additional information. No, this time a more direct look at his behavioral reaction when faced with the actuality of returning to Zimbabwe custody was necessary. There was no time left for dealing in hypothetical questions such as "What if you had to go back home?" Such questions had been posed to Gregory in the past and he had responded on an intellectual level each time: "I won't go!" or "I'd run away."

41

But what would really happen on an emotional level if Gregory were confronted with the situation? Would his functioning really deteriorate, as indicated in his responses to projective tests the week before? The State Department was going to find out the answer to that question within the next couple of days if it carried out its scheduled plans. I reasoned that it would be preferable to subject Gregory to this reality in as protective, nurturing, and supportive an environment as possible. If he did indeed react in an adverse manner, we would have the luxury of helping him to recover and cope without the immediate interference of others less sensitive to his psychological needs. I decided to risk presenting his transfer to him as a *fait accompli,* and then to observe his behavioral and emotional reaction.

The Sea Cliff office of St. Christopher-Ottilie is a small, three-story, turn-of-the-century frame house nestled in a rustic setting. It was at this site that the first St. Christopher's Home orphanage was located in the 1890s. It seemed incongruous to house the headquarters of the largest child-welfare agency in New York State in this serene, almost rural setting. Executive Director Robert Mc-Mahon and Assistant Executive Director Tom Ring were in McMahon's office when I arrived. Gregory and his caseworker, Stephanie Rothstein, were having lunch with another administrator, Gary Kipling, on an enclosed porch a few doors away. Gregory recognized and greeted me nonchalantly. He was totally relaxed, enjoying the attention of Stephanie and Gary. He certainly didn't appear as if he were on the verge of succumbing to a panic reaction. Leaving his present surroundings seemed the furthest thing from his mind. I did not relish the thought or welcome the role of destroying this temporary sense of tranquility.

Before starting with Gregory, I asked Stephanie to fill me in on his status since I last saw him on December 23. Following my evaluation that afternoon, Gregory had said goodbye to his sister Kim, who was then returned to the Zimbabwean mission. When I met briefly with Kim on the twenty-third, she had been ambivalent about returning to her mother and about leaving her brother, but she had finally decided to go. Kim felt quite guilt-ridden about being a participant in the abuse incidents, jeering at Gregory as her father had ordered. A family visit involving all three Tanaka children and Mrs. Tanaka had been attempted on Christmas Eve at the U.S. mission to the U.N. on First Avenue. Stephanie accompanied Gregory, who had been relatively calm until he was about to enter the room where his mother and sisters and officials from the Zimbabwean and U.S. missions awaited. Gregory pulled his coat over his head as he was led into the room. His shouts were clearly heard, despite being muffled by the coat.

"Why did you let Daddy hit me? Why didn't you call the police? Why did you laugh?"

Mrs. Tanaka did not respond directly to Gregory's questions. Instead she reacted defensively, discounting Gregory's allegations and denying the occurrence of abuse. There she was, surrounded by her nationals, her husband expelled from the country, while her child was publicly humiliating her. She could or would offer neither comfort nor explanation to her son. The atmosphere grew even more strained when Stephanie requested that the visit end. Gregory never lowered his coat from above his head until he was safely away from his mother.

Now Stephanie related how remarkably Gregory had recovered from the Christmas Eve visit. On Christmas Day he acted as though nothing had happened the day before. He continued to remain calm, cooperative, and affectionate throughout the next five days, and this, indeed, was the picture he was presenting as he chatted with Gary.

Once we were alone, Gregory and I engaged in some small talk. He was much more verbally and emotionally spontaneous than during our first meeting. He volunteered information about his past school history and a little about life in Zimbabwe. But his manner changed abruptly when the topic of his family troubles was raised. His responses were reduced to monotone, monosyllabic utterances as he reiterated his position that he wished to remain with his present foster mother and that he would not go back to Zimbabwe. We began talking about his difficult Christmas Eve visit, and then Gregory uttered a surprising statement.

"I want to see my mother again—I don't want to talk with her, I just want to see her."

I surmised that, contrary to previous indications, Gregory still desired contact with his mother and that there was a stronger bond between mother and child than was first apparent. Gregory showed a desire to clarify and resolve intensely conflicting feelings toward his mother. Feelings need expression; questions need answers. Gregory was not desirous of severing all of his familial ties after all. This was a highly significant revelation, which altered the direction of our efforts and of the entire case.

At this point Gregory was informed that a letter concerning his fate had been received. It was explained that he would be going to Zimbabwe to live with another family under the supervision of an agency similar to St. Christopher-Ottilie. Gregory's reaction was instant and dramatic. As I related in my psychological update,

> He climbed into a small transfer file and started to rock back and forth precipitously. As he rocked, he rolled his eyes and babbled and moaned, grasping his head in his hands. Any communication with the examiner was lost. . . . His reaction appeared to reflect an urgent, primitive defensive operation of withdrawing psychologically and emotionally from a reality that he could not face. Such regressive behavior, if sustained, would have warranted placement in a Residential Treatment Facility or hospitalization. It subsided, however, after Gregory was told that we would still do everything possible to allow him to stay. . . . It is imperative that Gregory not be moved from his present placement at this time. His behavior during the present evaluation suggests that he would be at even greater psychological risk than first estimated last week if a move were forced upon him prematurely.

Following the evaluation, Stephanie tearfully called me aside. In the three weeks since she had met Gregory she had grown emotionally attached, and was now suddenly considering the prospect that she'd be saying goodbye forever. She was scheduled to go away for several weeks and reasoned that she was letting Gregory down by not being present just when he needed her the most. She was uncertain about what to say. My suggestion was for her to avoid making any predictions or promises, but merely to tell him what she intended to do upon returning to New York later in January. Specifically, she told him that the first thing she'd do would be call up and find out how he was doing. That satisfied both Gregory and Stephanie, who then departed.

Bob, Tom, Gary, and I then met to review where we stood and what steps to take next. We decided that, no matter how bleak the outlook seemed, we would proceed, committed to the course of protecting Gregory against any threat to his psychological or physical well-being. I emphasized that Mrs. Tanaka had emerged as the key figure in establishing a direction for planning. The compelling evidence for the existence of a strong maternal bond demanded a re-examination of the initial Legal Aid Society move toward obtaining political asylum for Gregory. Clearly, a permanent stay in the United States ran counter to the indications that Gregory desired to repair at least some, if not most, of the damaged family ties. Yet continued pursuit of the request for asylum was the only recourse left to buy additional time to work with Gregory and to properly prepare him for his eventual return to Zimbabwe. Legal Aid was called to inform them of the results of the psychological update and to urge their continued efforts in Gregory's behalf.

Despite the decision to forge on, it still looked as though a transfer within the next day or two was unavoidable. Rather than subject Gregory's foster mother to the ordeal of last-minute pressures and a possible difficult scene at her home when government officials came for Gregory, it was decided that he'd stay at the nearby home of Gary Kipling and his family. Gregory had developed a positive feeling for Gary during the time they had spent together earlier in the day, and was therefore not hesitant about accompanying him. As all of us wished each other a happy New Year, we felt less than totally defeated and were buoyed by the conviction that we had done all that was humanly possible.

As I drove home, I put on a cassette tape that was given to me for the holidays by my sons, Jimmy, Adam, and Matthew. It was a tape of the most popular recordings of Don McLean, one of my favorite recording artists. One McLean song, originally recorded by

Perry Como, captured the moment for me and grew to symbolize the courageous battle that Gregory and other victims of child abuse silently wage on a daily basis. The song, "And I Love You So," is one usually associated with romantic love; but as I listened, its meaning broadened for me to include any deep, healing love born of prior painful, personal experience.

> And I love you so, the people ask me how;
> How I've lived 'til now, I tell them I don't know . . .
> And yes, I know how loveless life can be,
> The shadows follow me and the night won't set me free.
> But I don't let the evening get me down,
> Now that you're around me.

As I heard these lyrics, I couldn't help but visualize how painfully alone and unloved an abused child must feel as he or she tries to fall asleep each night. Upon awakening the next morning, the child must quickly face the sobering reality that the night could not set him free. What positive effect, if any, does the expression of concern and love from virtual strangers (e.g., caseworkers, foster parents, psychologists, administrators) have on a child with such a history? Would the genuine caring that Gregory was now receiving, albeit briefly, be able to neutralize or reverse the perception of being unloved or uncared for in the past? Only time would tell.

9. New Year's Day Showdown

ON FRIDAY, January 1, 1988, Joe Carrieri was awakened by a call from Robert Wayburn, assistant corporation counsel for the City of New York, who was the legal representative of the city in this case. He requested that the transfer of Gregory into the physical custody of U.S. State Department officials be arranged for that afternoon. Apparently the government was eager to have this case over and done with on one of the quietest days of the year, lessening the likelihood of unforeseen, last-minute foul-ups or of media interference. Joe contacted Bob McMahon and Tom Ring, and all agreed that the transfer should occur at the Carrieri and Lynch law offices in Jericho, New York, rather than at the home where Gregory was staying. At this point, no one outside of St. Christopher-Ottilie administration and Joe were aware that Gregory had been moved from his foster home to the Kipling home the night before.

Joe called Gary and informed him of the scheduled 3:00 P.M. transfer. Gary decided that it would be best to say nothing to Gregory until the time for departure was near. When Joe called me, his opening greeting was right to the point.

"The die is cast. They're taking him today."

My heart sank. Months later, I learned that, for all the St. Christopher-Ottilie participants in this case, their trip to Joe's office that Friday afternoon was the absolute low emotional point of the entire affair. It felt almost as if we were about to give up an innocent child for execution. All that was scheduled to happen was our complying with the law in giving Gregory over to respected representatives of our own federal government. Were we alarmists, overacting to our own irrational fears? Was I overstating the psychological risks involved in forcibly returning Gregory at this time? How could we not have faith in the ultimate wisdom and judgment of the New York State courts and the United States Department of State? After all, none of us thought of ourselves as revolutionaries. We were law-abiding, established citizens. Yet, as the minutes ticked away, there was a growing consensus among us that our government was about to commit a grievous mistake. Despite our doubts, we proceeded in anticipation of fully complying with the instructions for the transfer; but providence and a young boy's strong will interceded.

Back on Long Island at the Kipling home in Freeport, some fifteen miles away from the Carrieri law office, Gregory was informed by Gary of the intended transfer and took matters into his own hands. Gary, the most soft-spoken and gentle of men, tried to reassure Gregory that he would be protected first by representatives of the U.S. government and later by representatives of the Zimbabwean government. Fear was etched on Gregory's young face, a face that just minutes earlier was smiling and carefree. He spoke softly.

"But I don't want to go . . . I want to stay here."

He resisted only slightly at this point, and Gary was able to coax him into the front passenger's seat of his car. Gary helped Gregory buckle his seat belt, then pulled out of the driveway. Gregory's fears rapidly escalated toward a panic state. Just as predicted in both psychological evaluations, his level of functioning in general and his reality-testing in particular dropped markedly. Without considering the extreme danger involved, Gregory unbuckled his seat belt and started to open the door of the car, which was by now heading toward the Meadowbrook Parkway. Gary pulled over, re-buckled Gregory's seat belt, and attempted to resume the journey. Within seconds, Gregory made another attempt to jump out of the moving vehicle.

Exasperated and frightened for his passenger's safety, Gary announced, "We're going back home."

The ordeal wasn't over when they arrived home. Gregory, mindful that another attempt to transport him might soon be made, ran from Gary's grasp as they entered the house. He dashed up to the second-floor master bedroom, where he began opening one of the windows. He was about to jump out when Gary and his wife, Joannie, caught him and held him.

"You can stop trying to get away. I'm not going to take you anywhere," said Gary.

Minutes passed before Gregory stopped struggling. His personal crisis was over for the time being.

Gary called Joe's office and informed Tom of the latest developments. He emphatically stated that he could not and would not attempt to force Gregory back in the car. He was told to sit tight and wait for further instructions.

Minutes later, two State Department officials, a middle-aged man and a somewhat younger woman, arrived at Joe Carrieri's law office. With cordial smiles, they expectantly asked to see Gregory. After a delay of a few seconds that seemed like hours, Bob McMahon began to describe the problem that had arisen. It took a little more time before the officials deduced that Gregory was neither present at the law office nor likely to appear soon. As all of us eased into Joe's law library, the mood and posture of the man and woman transformed to reflect dismay, anger, and, eventually on the part of the woman, near panic. She was anything but understanding of the plight of poor Gregory. She either didn't hear or failed to comprehend that Gregory had endangered his own life to avoid being turned over to the Zimbabwean government. Instead, she challenged the others at the table.

"What do you mean he wouldn't come? Why wasn't he just carried out and held?" she barked.

"Madam, don't you see? The boy's life was in danger. It wasn't worth the risk," Tom answered.

The woman persisted. "You were ordered to bring that child here. How dare you disregard the government's orders!"

Undaunted, but becoming enraged, Tom countered, "Just who do you think you're talking to? You haven't heard a word that's been said."

The woman's State Department colleague interjected, "The bottom line is that you are not complying with what has been ordered."

"We tried, but we've been prevented from complying," Joe stated.

"You can be held in contempt of court. You may be guilty of insubordination to the United States government" was the woman's stern and threatening response to Joe.

I had never seen Tom in this light in the eight years I had known him. A native of Ireland, Tom had spent a good portion of his young adult life in the priesthood. He had left the clergy and started a family as a middle-aged man. Tom's human sensitivity could be found in his actions and his words. His notable British accent lent an air of distinction to whatever he said. For the most part, however, he was restrained in his pursuit of issues or causes dear to him—not out of any sense of apathy, but because of his reserved British style. In the present exchange, Tom's passion for what was right could not be contained in the face of the remarks of the woman from the State Department. His outrage at the indecency of what was transpiring helped all of us to define the moral imperative to persevere.

Clearly, this was getting nowhere. I began to speculate quietly that the two officials were convinced that we were intentionally misleading them and actively resisting compliance with the orders to transfer Gregory. Their erroneous belief was fueled by a phone call they had made earlier in the day to the foster home where Gregory had resided during December. When the foster mother explained that Gregory was no longer staying with her and that she didn't know his whereabouts, they suspected duplicity on the part of the St. Christopher-Ottilie administrators. Now that he hadn't been brought for the transfer, they were apparently convinced that they were being "jerked around." If this scenario was correct, then their almost tragi-comic behavior could be understood. Without such an explanation, one would have to surmise that they were such hardened bureaucrats that they no longer possessed the capacity to empathize with a panic-stricken, desperate young child.

Time passed as the two officials took turns shuttling to the car phone in the State Department vehicle downstairs, communicating with their superiors in Washington. One fact became quite clear. There was virtually no trust at all between the State Department officials and the St. Christopher-Ottilie people. My own disillusionment with this sample of our government at work was growing. If we were to be found guilty of being in contempt of the law, then perhaps we must follow the tenets of a "higher law."

This impasse continued until 6:30 P.M., when a call from the Legal Aid Society delivered some surprising news. They had been successful in reaching Jack B. Weinstein, chief judge of the Eastern District Federal Court, who had heard a telephone appeal and had issued a temporary stay preventing the United States government from forcibly taking physical custody of Gregory. The stay had been granted for the purpose of hearing the merits of the Legal Aid Society's argument that Gregory should be allowed to have his petition for asylum acted upon by the U.S. Immigration and Naturalization Service before a final determination regarding a forcible return to State Department custody was made. The stay had been granted until the next day, Saturday, January 2. The judge directed that all parties be present at his Long Island home for a hearing.

10. Gregory Becomes a Federal Case

G REGORY'S CASE graduated to the federal level on a crisp, sunny Saturday morning, the second of January. Bob McMahon, Gary Kipling, and I remained in Joe's car just outside of Judge Weinstein's North Shore home, while Joe Carrieri went in to inquire about procedure. Since St. Christopher-Ottilie's participation at the hearing was supposed to be as *amicus curiae* (friend of the court), it was not known whether any of us besides Joe would be welcomed inside and asked to participate.

All of us were heartily welcomed. Judge Weinstein, a tall, distinguished, and soft-spoken gentleman, greeted us at the door as Mrs. Weinstein took our coats. We were escorted through the living room to the dining room table, where the hearing would take place. The dining room overlooked Long Island Sound and offered a beautiful view of the New York City skyline in the distance. If nothing else, this was a marvelous setting for pursuing a cause that we thought had been lost—first on December 22, when the family court first ordered Gregory discharged to the State Department, and then on January 1, when Gregory was just a fifteen-minute ride from being placed into the custody of State Department officials. Despite the magnitude and tension of the moment, all four of the St. Christopher-Ottilie participants appeared calm and determined. I will never forget the serene and confident expression on Bob's face as he gazed at the view just prior to the initiation of the proceedings. If there was anxiety present, it didn't show. Bob knew that he was leading an honorable and just cause, so there was really nothing to be apprehensive about. His demeanor and expression had a calming effect on the rest of the St. Christopher-Ottilie contingent.

Seated around or near the dining room table were Judge Weinstein, U.S. Attorney Igou Allbray, U.S. Immigration and Naturalization Service Attorney Scott Blackman, Legal Aid Society attorneys Henry Weintraub and Elizabeth Johanns, Assistant Corporation Counsel Robert Wayburn, a court stenographer, and the four of us from St. Christopher-Ottilie. Mrs. Weinstein was an interested spectator who took great interest in the proceedings. She also served coffee in her capacity as gracious hostess.

Henry Weintraub of the Legal Aid Society presented the arguments that were the basis for the civil action. Essentially, the complaint asserted that Gregory's federal statutory and regulatory rights were "being violated by the government's refusal to follow its procedures while his asylum application was pending." It asserted that his procedural due-process rights under the Fifth Amendment to the United States Constitution and under federal immigration laws and regulations were being violated by the government's refusal to grant him a deportation hearing prior to his forcible and involuntary removal from the United States. Weintraub requested that the Eastern District Federal Court assume jurisdiction and enter a temporary restraining order preventing the federal government from removing Gregory from the United States before affording him a deportation hearing, and preventing the federal government from removing Gregory from the United States pending a determination of his asylum application. Preliminary and permanent injunctive relief were sought.

U.S. Attorney Allbray, a reserved, distinguished-looking gentleman who appeared to be of Middle Eastern descent, curtly responded with the government's position. He cited the opinion that, under the laws of diplomatic immunity, the State Department is assigned sole responsibility for safeguarding the internationally accepted rights of diplomats and their families.

He argued that, "because of the diplomatic immunity of the child and his parents, courts of the United States lack the authority to prevent the transfer of physical custody of Gregory to the Zimbabwean authorities." He also noted the possibility that, "if the court did not honor the claims based on diplomatic immunity in this case, the courts of a foreign nation could, acting under the principle of reciprocity, exercise jurisdiction over an American child under a claim that the child had been abused."

It was then my turn to testify. I found myself in a peculiar position. I was there as a supporter of the Legal Aid Society's efforts to prevent the government from taking immediate custody of Gregory. I did not, however, support a plan involving permanent asylum in the United States. The evaluation of December 31 convinced me that, given the maternal bonds that were evident as well as the implicit need for Gregory to resolve conflicting feelings toward his mother, long-range efforts should be in the direction of repairing rather than completely severing significant family relationships. Yet the essence of the Legal Aid Society's claim was that Gregory was being denied due process in applying for asylum. My position, and that of St. Christopher-Ottilie, was by now crystallized and defined. We needed time. Time was needed to prepare Gregory for a return to his homeland that was all but inevitable. The action of Legal Aid was helping in that regard, but I began my remarks by making it clear that permanent asylum was not necessarily the ultimate answer for Gregory.

I testified that "our objective is to return the child to the care of his nationals in a manner that is consistent with preventing decompensation or deterioration of his mental health and/or with preventing action on his part that would be dangerous to himself."

I likened Gregory to a "ticking time bomb" that had to be carefully defused. If we failed to proceed cautiously (e.g., if we forcibly and prematurely removed him to Zimbabwe), then the likelihood of an adverse and prolonged emotional reaction would be great. I attempted to explain Gregory's terror of anyone connected with Zimbabwe by comparing him to a child who has a generalized fear of dogs. Although such fear might have its origin in a traumatic experience with only one dog, it can spread irrationally to encompass all sizes and breeds of dogs. In such an instance, one cannot simply tell the child to stop being afraid or to refrain from panicking. The only way to diminish the child's fears and vulnerability to a panic reaction is to gradually desensitize him to what is not really dangerous. I had begun to offer a concrete plan for how this might be accomplished when Judge Weinstein stopped me.

"I've heard enough," he declared.

A short break followed. Bob, Joe, and Gary congratulated me on my presentation, but I was frustrated over not being allowed to give a summary of my treatment recommendations. I wanted the judge to understand that, rather than looking for an indefinite, interminable period of time, we were seeking just six to eight weeks to accomplish our objective. On the other hand, I was heartened by the attentiveness of all the participants to what I had to say. Of all present, however, no one was more attentive than the judge's wife. During my testimony, she positioned herself at the door between the kitchen and dining room, directly across from where I was seated. Consequently, the most direct eye contact that I shared with anyone during my testimony was with Mrs. Weinstein. The thought registered: "Why was she so interested in these proceedings?" During the break, I found the answer. She approached me, stating how interested she was in my presentation. She explained that she was a retired psychiatric social worker who had helped found a major child guidance center in Nassau County. Child welfare had long been an area of professional and personal interest to her. She joked how most in-home hearings that she had been privy to had been less than stimulating to her.

"They involve things like railroad disputes."

Following the break, two other State Department attorneys arrived, and there was much whispering among colleagues. Judge Weinstein was prepared to issue his decision and, a hush fell over the room. The judge initially spoke very softly, in almost inaudible tones; then his wife interrupted.

"Speak up, I can't hear you. The people want to know."

This elicited chuckles from everyone, but the judge's ensuing comments failed to amuse us.

"The reason for the diplomatic immunity in these cases is very clear. As a matter of reciprocity, it is essential under the law of nations that diplomats be free to leave with their families at any time. . . . The child must be turned over to the United States. St. Christopher's is without valid custody of the child."

We were thus denied our requests for a temporary restraining order, a preliminary injunction, and a permanent injunction. Judge Weinstein ordered that physical custody of Gregory would be turned over to the United States at 1:00 P.M., Monday, January 4, 1988, but he added an important qualifier.

He looked at Allbray and said, "It is up to you to make whatever arrangements are necessary to get the child. It is not St. Christopher's responsibility to deliver the child to you. It's up to the government to pick him up and to ensure his safety."

The hearing was over. For the first time all morning, Igou Allbray cracked a big, wide smile. Colleagues were congratulating him and each other for their accomplishment. I felt defeated.

As I was rising from my chair, I looked up to Mrs. Weinstein, who was rushing toward me. She was deeply moved as she frantically inquired, "What's going to happen to the boy? Who will be taking responsibility for him when he's moved?"

I gazed in the direction of Allbray, standing next to Judge Weinstein. "That's out of our hands now. They took responsibility away from us."

Mrs. Weinstein was not satisfied. "Something has to be done to make sure he's treated correctly. A professional has to be involved. Talk to them!"

By now Bob had joined us and had heard Mrs. Weinstein's impassioned plea. Her remarks were like a shot of adrenaline. She was energizing us to further action, just when we were feeling that all was lost. We walked over to Allbray, who was still all aglow from his victory and, perhaps as a consequence, even more receptive to our request.

With Judge Weinstein in earshot, Bob forcefully argued that the State Department must enlist the help of a mental health professional to monitor and assume responsibility for Gregory's emotional state. The day before, two bureaucrats had been sent to pick up Gregory and the results could have been catastrophic.

"You must have a psychiatrist or a psychologist involved," Bob concluded.

Allbray acquiesced as Judge Weinstein nodded affirmatively. He assured us and the judge that immediate efforts would be made to retain someone in the mental health field. It was clear to all present that the judge expected the State Department to take any and all necessary precautions to ensure the child's safety and well-being during the transfer.

As Bob, Joe, Gary, and I rode back to Joe's office, we reviewed the day's events. We had done all we could have done, but only one thought now crossed my mind: "I hate losing."

When we arrived at the office, Joe received a phone call from a Cable News Network contact who requested an interview concerning the hearing and Gregory's status. Up to this point, St. Christopher-Ottilie had been virtually anonymous as far as the media were concerned. Newspaper articles during December referred to us as a child care agency or foster care agency, but the agency's name had not been used, nor had any of our names. None of us sought publicity for ourselves, and it was questionable whether publicity for the agency would be viewed favorably or unfavorably within the child welfare system. Joe asked Bob how he felt about doing an interview. Bob begged off, but encouraged me to do so if I felt comfortable. This came as somewhat of a surprise to me, for I had assumed that Bob would just as soon shun any agency publicity that might be too controversial. I had been wrong. My reaction was one of anticipatory excitement. I felt that going on the air with Joe would give us the opportunity to publicize the informal agreement reached with Allbray regarding his securing a psychiatrist or psychologist. It would be a means of keeping the State Department honest.

After Bob and Gary left, Joe contacted Bob Wayburn, the corporation counsel, to see if he had any problem with our being interviewed by CNN. Wayburn called back a few minutes later to say that his boss, the director of the city's Human Resources Administration, was against the interview. His reasons were vague, but Joe did not attempt to challenge the decision. He didn't want to antagonize the city agency.

11. State Sends a Consultant

Igou Allbray was true to his word. Within twenty-four hours of the hearing at Judge Weinstein's home, he had arranged to have Gregory seen by a child psychiatrist. Dr. Don Heacock, director of child and adolescent psychiatry at Lincoln Medical and Mental Health Center, with a private Park Avenue practice as well, was dispatched to the Kipling home on Sunday afternoon, the third of January. He was accompanied by the same two State Department officials who had been present at Joe Carrieri's office on New Year's Day. This time, the mood was light and the atmosphere was friendly and cordial. Dr. Heacock, a kindly black gentleman of late-middle age, asked me to accompany him to the kitchen to meet Gregory. After several minutes it was evident that Gregory felt comfortable enough to be left alone with Dr. Heacock. I returned to the living room, where I rejoined the State Department officials, Gary, and Tom Ring, who was there as well. About forty minutes later, Dr. Heacock returned and began to share his observations with the rest of us.

"Gregory seems to have above-average intelligence. He's a charming little fellow and appears to be normal in most respects. I find no overt pathology, but he's extremely frightened of being returned to his father. He requires a 'therapeutic transition,' during which he can learn to trust a new caretaker."

Dr. Heacock did not define or elaborate on what he specifically meant by "therapeutic transition," but I immediately concurred that this was what we had been seeking as well. We all agreed that we did not wish to have Gregory traumatized by the method or the timing of the transfer.

I breathed a sigh of relief. Until that moment I had been the only mental health professional whose findings and opinions had been debated at the center of this growing international controversy. I was somewhat apprehensive about the prospect of being publicly challenged by the State Department psychiatrist, who could have refuted my findings and conclusions. But now the State Department's own psychiatrist appeared to be concurring with my recommendation to proceed cautiously and therapeutically. From that point on, I adopted a variation of Dr. Heacock's term and repeatedly referred to the need for a "therapeutic transfer."

As the discussion progressed, it soon became evident that all was not as rosy as it first appeared. Dr. Heacock was vague as Tom attempted to pin him down on his specific thoughts about how a therapeutic transfer might be accomplished.

The woman from the State Department became a bit impatient as she interjected, "Look, we're all under the legal constraint to move the child tomorrow, no matter what it takes."

A stony silence ensued. The unmistakable implication was that force would be used if necessary. Just like that, the concept of a therapeutic transfer was shoved aside. It was approaching 7:00 P.M., and the guests were about to leave.

As I shook Dr. Heacock's hand, I asked, as an afterthought, "So you'll be here tomorrow when Gregory leaves?"

Dr. Heacock hesitated and looked puzzled. "No one said anything about my coming back. As a matter of fact, I will be instructing a class tomorrow."

I was aghast. The whole purpose of the State Department's hiring a psychiatrist was to ensure that Gregory's fragile psychological state could be monitored and overseen by a professional after I left the picture. What was the purpose of sending Dr. Heacock out to see Gregory if his thoughts about a therapeutic transfer were to be minimized or overlooked and if he would not accept professional responsibility for overseeing the transfer itself.

Was the State Department merely placating and patronizing us by sending a psychiatrist on Sunday without the slightest intention of using him thereafter? Or did Allbray and other State Department officials fail to comprehend, appreciate, or care at all about the fragile psychological condition that Gregory was really in? I feared that the answer to both questions was yes.

The night was young. There was important work to do. Calls were made to Bob McMahon and Henry Weintraub at the Legal Aid Society to inform them of the latest turn of events. It was unanimously deduced that the State Department was quite prepared to ignore the advice of its own consulting psychiatrist and to betray the agreement made with Judge Weinstein, Bob, and me at the conclusion of Saturday's hearing. Weintraub said that he would request another conference with Judge Weinstein the next morning with the hope that this new information would prompt the judge to modify his order transferring physical custody of Gregory to the United States government at 1:00 P.M. Later in the evening, Bob called me at home to advise me that a conference was indeed scheduled for Monday morning in Judge Weinstein's courtroom. He asked me to attend as an observer, to be on hand just in case Legal Aid needed me to clarify anything.

Our moods at the moment were a study in contrast. I was doing a slow burn over what I perceived as deception being put to use by the State Department. Bob, on the other hand, was like the cat who ate the canary. He was strongly optimistic about what might happen the next day in Judge Weinstein's courtroom. Did he know something that I didn't know? Perhaps!

I was the sole representative of St. Christopher-Ottilie at the conference on the morning of Monday, January 4. The judge projected a far more formal and official image in his large, imposing courtroom than he had at his home. He sat at a conference table in the middle of the room rather than on the bench. I seated myself in the first row of spectator seats directly behind Igou Allbray, who was directly across the table from Judge Weinstein. If the judge were to look beyond Allbray's left ear, he would have me in his line of vision. Also seated in the courtroom were numerous government officials and attorneys, as well as a number of news reporters.

Weintraub spoke first, giving the basis for his motion to modify

Judge Weinstein's prior order. He referred to our phone conversation of the night before, in which I had described my talk with Dr. Heacock.

"Dr. Gries reports that Dr. Heacock's findings were consistent with his, and that both agreed that a therapeutic transfer is required. Comments made by State Department officials at the conclusion of yesterday's meeting strongly suggest that Dr. Heacock's recommendations will not be followed; that abrupt, forcible transfer will be attempted today as originally planned."

Allbray stood up and disputed the accuracy of statements attributed to Dr. Heacock. The doctor, he said, had suggested only that "a therapeutic transfer would be *preferable*. He didn't say, however, that it was necessary."

When I heard this, I reflexively slapped my forehead with my hand, creating a noticeable sound, and I looked to the ceiling in a state of disbelief. I couldn't believe what I was hearing. This testimony by a ranking attorney for the U.S. government, given right there before a federal judge, was clearly at odds with what I recalled of my conversation with Dr. Heacock. I was dismayed. I was a product of the 1950s, when Eisenhower was president and law and order and government officials were respected; assassinations, Vietnam, and Watergate were years away. No one growing up in the '50s ever dreamed that such nightmares could occur in the good old USA. My main concern in those days was whether or not the Brooklyn Dodgers would ever beat the Yankees in the World Series. Now I was facing the stark reality that either times had changed drastically or my perception of things had undergone a metamorphosis.

Weintraub asked to speak again. "Your Honor, not only is Dr. Heacock's advice being ignored, but he indicated to Dr. Gries that he has no plan to be present when Gregory is taken into the physical custody of the government."

Judge Weinstein, who must have noticed my reaction, addressed Allbray. "Is Dr. Heacock here in the courtroom?"

"No, Your Honor, he's not."

"Do you have a written report from Dr. Heacock?"

"No, Your Honor," was the reply.

"Can we reach him by telephone? Do you have his number?"

The judge was becoming noticeably impatient. A brief recess was called while futile attempts were made to reach Dr. Heacock by phone. Afterward, the judge informed the parties of his decision.

Judge Weinstein denied the motion to delay the time of transfer of Gregory's custody. Furthermore, he denied a motion to stay his order until the New York State Court of Appeals had an opportunity to review a decision of the appellate division concerning the initial family court order to transfer custody to the State Department. He declared, "The New York State Court of Appeals has no more jurisdiction than the family court of the state. . . . All state courts are stayed and enjoined from proceeding in this action. That order is issued on two grounds. One, as a matter of diplomatic concern, diplomatic immunity, the state courts have no jurisdiction. Two, the order is issued in order to protect the jurisdiction of the federal court."

From a legal standpoint, Judge Weinstein was holding his ground. He was adhering to a strict-constructionist interpretation of diplomatic immunity, with no room for exceptions or extenuating circumstances. Yet despite the content of his decision, somehow I received the impression that he was on our side, that he was far more sympathetic to our cause and to Gregory's needs than he had shown on Saturday. With a twinkle in his eye, he seemed to derive some degree of satisfaction over how difficult the State Department's job would be in attempting to take custody. He rattled off legal procedural requirements, emphasizing the fact that it was the government's responsibility—and no one else's—to secure Gregory's custody. He reminded Allbray that a writ of habeas corpus and an order to show cause (why the child should not forcibly be taken from the Kipling home) were necessary. He emphasized the fact that Kipling would be required to play no role in restraining Gregory in the event Gregory resisted.

Judge Weinstein turned to Weintraub and reminded the Legal Aid lawyer that this decision could be appealed. He spelled out exactly what would be required for the appeal to be made, as though he were prepared to take Weintraub by the hand and walk him through the process. I had the distinct impression that Judge Weinstein very much wanted his decision to be appealed.

•

The hallway outside the courtroom was crowded with government officials, spectators, and members of the media. I stood off to the side, taking it all in with fascination. I watched as Bob Wayburn and Henry Weintraub were questioned by a television news reporter. Suddenly, a young woman approached me and introduced herself as a reporter for *Newsday,* a Long Island daily. Any hesitancy about going on the record had been shattered by the events of the previous forty-eight hours. Statements being made by the State Department were erroneous, if not outright falsehoods. The legal battle was definitely being lost; possibly it had already been lost. The only hope for Gregory, the only remaining source of protection for him now, seemed to rest with public opinion. Bob McMahon must have realized that the day before when he went on record in a newspaper interview. Now I felt free—and even compelled—to do the same.

The reporter asked a few brief questions about my opinion regarding what had transpired in the courtroom. My answers were as brief as her questions, and before I knew it, she was gone. Just then, Igou Allbray emerged from the courtroom. He headed directly toward me. There had been no prior acknowledgment between us that morning, but now he was very purposefully making his way in my direction. I took a deep breath as he nodded his head and spoke.

"Why don't you just drop everything? Let it end. You can call it off."

I gave one of the broadest, phoniest smiles of my entire life. I muttered something to the effect that we had to do what we had to do; but frankly, I was too stunned and flabbergasted to make an intelligent reply or to remember what I actually said. Here we were, getting soundly and consistently beaten in every legal confrontation since December 22, and yet Allbray approached me as though we had the upper hand.

For the first time, I fully realized that we had much more leverage than had been apparent. The reason for this was all around us in the form of the media—the fourth estate. By now, the watchful eye of the media had fully entered the fray, television sound trucks and all. No longer could the State Department hope to whisk or drag off Gregory anonymously and thus be rid of its diplomatic crisis. No longer could it simply ignore or discount the pleas of Gregory's law guardian, Erwin Weisberg, or his caseworker at St. Christopher-Ottilie, Stephanie Rothstein, to proceed cautiously in planning for this extremely frightened and traumatized child. No longer could the truth be easily skirted. Ultimately, like it or not, the State Department and the government in general are accountable to the public. With the help of the media, the public was now being made part of the equation.

Henry Weintraub excused himself from the discussion with the newsman, Christopher Jones of Fox-TV. He was in a hurry to arrange for the appeal of Judge Weinstein's order. This left Bob Wayburn alone with Jones.

Wayburn called me over and introduced me to the reporter. I described the sources and form of Gregory's fear, giving some anecdotal material as well. Without warning, Jones asked me to accompany him to the lobby of the Federal Court Building, where his camera crew was waiting. Prior to that moment, my television exposure had consisted of sitting with my wife-to-be, Susanne, in front-row seats at the Les Crane show on ABC-TV in the '60s and marching around Ebbets Field in my little league uniform in the early '50s. (My parents swore that they spotted me and my brother Phil on the 13-inch screen.) I felt a rush of adrenaline, but there really was insufficient time to get nervous. Just like that, I was being interviewed on television. It seemed like a dream, but it wasn't. It was very real, and there was now a very real opportunity to tell Gregory's story directly to the public and thereby receive much-needed support.

On camera, I explained how Gregory's fear of his father had generalized to all Zimbabweans. "For Gregory, a return to anyone from Zimbabwe would be tantamount to being returned directly to his father."

Chris Jones ended his segment by quoting Yogi Berra in referring to Gregory's legal chances: "Today, Gregory learned one more thing about America: In American courts, 'It ain't over 'til it's over.'"

After the interview, I rushed to my car and headed for Gary Kipling's house in Freeport. In the back of mind was the 1:00 P.M. transfer time set by Judge Weinstein on Saturday. There was no way of knowing whether Henry Weintraub or his colleagues would be successful at winning another stay through the U.S. Court of Appeals. If a transfer was going to take place, I wanted to be there to lend whatever support I could to Gregory, as well as to Gary. While driving along the Brooklyn-Queens Expressway, I observed the second encouraging sign of the day, which gave a message of hope, if not optimism.

The first sign had been implicit in Allbray's attitude and demeanor as he approached me in the hallway outside the courtroom. The second sign was a well-formed, crystal-clear rainbow rising from the roadway just ahead of me and to my left. Melting snow along the shoulder in conjunction with a sparkling winter sun created the necessary conditions for the rainbow, but I had never before seen anything like it on a city highway. "Somehow, things are going to work out," I thought.

All was quiet when I arrived at Gary's home. The 1:00 P.M. deadline came and went, and as the afternoon wore on Gary and I surmised that there would be no attempt to take Gregory into custody that day. Gregory, ever vigilant to what was transpiring, sensed that nothing was going to happen and relaxed noticeably. He gleefully played with Gary and Joannie's two boys, Jeremy and Adam, as if he had not a care in the world. How quickly he was able to reverse gears!

Suddenly, at 4:00 P.M., there was a knock on the front door. It was a U.S. marshal. He served Gary with a writ of habeas corpus and an order to show cause why the child should not be taken from him. This had a sobering effect on both Gary and me. It appeared that the State Department was actually prepared to follow through with its plan to resort to force and strong-arm tactics if necessary in gaining physical custody of Gregory. One question entered my mind: "Would they dare do this in front of the TV cameras?"

Upstairs, Gregory seemed to be aware of occurrences but confused about what was happening. He knew that at a moment's notice he could be whisked away into the hands of others who, he feared, would send him back to his father. He had had several close calls already to prove this possibility. When the marshal left, Gregory came downstairs and appeared to be relieved, as were we. He had this uncanny knack of momentarily sweeping things out of his mind and returning to routine mood and behavior. That night, however, he refused to get undressed for bed. He slept on the floor near a door leading to the backyard. He was prepared for a quick getaway should there be a surprise in the middle of the night. Such was the state of psychological terror under which Gregory was trying to function.

12. The Guardian *Ad Litem*

WHILE THE U.S. marshal was performing his duty at Gary Kipling's home, Henry Weintraub, Elizabeth Johanns, Janet Fink, Lenore Gittis, and the rest of the Legal Aid Society team steadfastly continued to perform their duties. By 1:00 P.M. they had filed a notice of appeal with the United States Court of Appeals for the Second Circuit and had moved for a preliminary injunction pending appeal. Within two hours, a three-judge appellate panel had heard oral arguments from both parties and ordered that the status quo regarding Gregory be maintained pending appeal. This marked the third eleventh-hour reprieve for Gregory, who had been similarly within minutes of being taken into the government's physical custody on December 23 and on January 1. It was getting to feel like one of those old 1930s movies, where the prisoner on death row is saved by a last-minute pardon from the governor.

The panel noted and was dismayed by a glaring omission in Gregory's status. Throughout all the legal maneuvering of the preceding two weeks, Gregory technically had been a minor without a guardian. Once the family court judge ruled on December 23 that the State Department should have custody of Gregory, the child technically was no longer in foster care and was, therefore, not the responsibility of the city's Special Services for Children. The city and St. Christopher-Ottilie had continued to function as though Gregory were a duly placed foster child, but he wasn't. He was in a kind of legal no-man's land—neither in the foster care system nor in the physical custody of the State Department. As a minor, he needed a temporary guardian to act in his best interests until the question of legal and physical custody was resolved. Action was remanded to Judge Weinstein for the limited purpose of appointing a guardian, referred to as the *guardian ad litem*, who would represent Gregory during the appeal period and in any proceedings before the Immigration and Naturalization Service.

On Tuesday, January 5, Judge Weinstein, over the objections of the federal government, appointed Robert McMahon, executive director of St. Christopher-Ottilie, Services for Children and Families, as Gregory's guardian *ad litem*. This was a most significant step in the direction of safeguarding Gregory's rights and best interests. Most important, it gave legitimacy to all of us working with Bob in Gregory's behalf. It ensured that, whatever the outcome, at least some semblance of due process would be afforded. Gregory now had a guardian, a concerned, caring, surrogate parent to see to it that his interests were protected to the full extent of the law.

Who would have predicted that Bob McMahon would find himself in this position at the center of an international storm, and taking on the federal government? Bob had always impressed me as a highly intelligent and most diligent administrator who knew how to understand and to use the system to further his objectives. With his computer-like facility for digesting and applying factual information in his no-nonsense, low-key style, he could easily be mistaken for a successful CEO in corporate industry. He did not seem like a leader in the child welfare field or a maverick ready to buck the system. How projections and images can be misleading!

Bob came to what was then called St. Christopher's Home in June 1973 to become the first layman to head the relatively small agency. After spending eighteen years as a brother in Holy Cross, a Catholic religious order, he had decided to leave the clergy and marry. A Notre Dame graduate, he spent a number of years teaching in the order, which included a stint in Rome. He later became director of Pius XII, a residential center for boys in upstate New York, where he developed an innovative drug-rehabilitation program. This was in 1970, long before such programs were fashionable or commonplace.

When Bob arrived at St. Christopher's in 1973, the agency served fewer than three hundred children in a shelter and in foster homes on Long Island. In less than fifteen years he had molded it into the largest child care agency in New York State, serving over 2,500 children and families a year. In 1988, the agency boasted three burgeoning community service centers for coordinating foster care services throughout the metropolitan area; a residential treatment center for severely disturbed young children; a residential treatment facility (fully accredited by the Joint Commission of Agencies and Hospitals) for serving dual-diagnosed adolescents; many group homes for children with psychiatric disturbances, conduct disorders, or mental retardation; programs for unwed mothers and the homeless; and several comprehensive prevention programs helping to keep potential clients out of foster care. Aside from the enormous scope of the services provided, the agency enjoyed a fine reputation for the quality of its efforts. Bob was often thought of first when the city or state had a new program that needed to be developed. To say that Bob was a doer or an achiever would be an understatement. Yet he was never one to seek confrontation or publicity. He always epitomized "establishment," whether it was as a school board member, church leader, or homeowner with his wife, Kathy, and their three girls.

Bob's intelligence, knowledge, and experience in child care, his doggedness and persistence, his faith in adhering to the moral high road regardless of the consequences, his calm, rational temperament, and his ability to read the system and make the necessary adjustments for mid-course corrections made him the ideal selection for Gregory's guardian *ad litem*. In order to succeed, Bob would have to play the role of quarterback, which he always did so well. But now he was facing an unfamiliar adversary with unfamiliar defensive alignments. Instead of dealing with the familiar city foster care system or state social services department, he was now calling "automatics" in the arena of national politics.

13. Getting Political

BOB MCMAHON had not been deluded by the ups and downs of the legal battle over Gregory. No matter how heartening a particular favorable decision may have been, he knew that it would continue to be an uphill battle in court, with almost insurmountable odds against winning. The issue of diplomatic immunity simply extended this case beyond the scope and jurisdiction of any American court. The only thing we seemed to be accomplishing was buying time. But buying time for what? What could possibly be gained by dragging out the case for a few more days? The answer was that there was everything to gain—not in court, but in the political and public domains.

In our system of government, no one branch can function in a vacuum. The State Department certainly gave the impression that it could function autonomously when it came to matters concerning the treatment of foreign diplomats. In fact, the State Department did—and does—possess the legal mandate to independently carry out all diplomatic functions, including protecting the rights of diplomats under the convention of diplomatic immunity. The courts, thus far, had supported such a notion wholeheartedly. If the matter was that simple, however, why had Igou Allbray beseeched me to call off the whole thing outside Judge Weinstein's courtroom? Was Allbray fully aware that, up to that point, only two of the players in our checks-and-balances system of government had been heard from? The two protagonists thus far were the State

Department, representing the executive branch, and the courts, representing the judicial branch. The legislative branch, Congress, had not yet been heard from, but its role in this matter, if it had any, was still unclear. The fourth estate, the press, representing the public and public opinion, was just beginning to establish its role, but was it going to be too little too late?

With his appointment as guardian *ad litem* out of the way, Bob's attention turned to enlisting and nurturing the support and help of Congress and the press.

Without knowing which senators or congressmen would be most sympathetic to our case, Bob contacted the offices of both U.S. senators from New York, Patrick Moynihan and Al D'Amato. Contacts were also made with a number of New York congressmen. The most enthusiastic support came from Senator Moynihan and Congressman Bill Ackerman. There were numerous phone calls between Moynihan's assistant, Paul Stockton, in Washington and Bob in Sea Cliff. Stockton, a young and effervescent man with a delightful sense of humor, seemed unjaded by his experiences in Washington. He maintained a cautious skepticism about political statements and actions, while always retaining an air of optimism. Once he understood what our intentions were, he had little difficulty communicating our position to Senator Moynihan. On Wednesday, January 6, the senator issued a public statement in support of St. Christopher-Ottilie and Bob's efforts. He didn't hedge; he was fully in our corner.

Stockton's next task was to educate the right people in the State Department concerning our position and objectives. It was important for people with clout, perhaps with access to Secretary of State George Schultz, to understand that we were not interested in political asylum for Gregory, the appeals court litigation notwithstanding. Our goal was to rekindle the notion of a 120-day humanitarian leave, as originally discussed back on December 23. Such a leave can be granted by the Department of Justice in a case where a foreigner's condition does not permit travel, but it necessitates emergency treatment. This was an accurate description of Gregory's situation. On the same day that Senator Moynihan's statement was released, Stockton spoke with Richard Shifter, assistant secretary of state for human rights, who said that he'd support the move for a humanitarian leave. Shifter used a slightly different term, "humanitarian parole," with a time frame of only three to five weeks. Of course, it remained for the Justice Department and the State Department to agree on a unified approach. What was important, however, was that there were now open lines of communication, albeit indirect, between Bob and some prominent congressional figures as well as officials at Justice and State at the under-secretary's level. The number of actors and the size of the stage for this drama were growing by the hour.

Two other unbelievable events occurred in Washington that day, demonstrating how unpredictable things had become. Senator Jesse Helms of North Carolina, a ranking member of the Senate Foreign Relations Committee, issued a public blockbuster. He intended to introduce legislation that would make Gregory a United States citizen and permit him to stay here for the rest of his life. Gregory was assuredly not alone anymore.

The second event occurred in two parts. On the morning of the sixth, President Ronald Reagan was quoted in news reports as being very sympathetic to Gregory's plight. His position as stated was that no steps would be taken that would jeopardize Gregory's well-being. Bob, Tom Ring, Gary Kipling, Yara Fernandez, and I were at Sea Cliff discussing a treatment plan for Gregory when St. Christopher-Ottilie Foster care directors Mary Odom and Maria Cockinos called to inform us of the president's statement. We were euphoric! It seemed that within the short span of a few days our message had successfully reached the president of the United States. This "high" was quickly shattered later in the day. On the evening news reports there was no mention of the president's humanitarian position. Instead, a White House spokesman reiterated the previous State Department position that, because of diplomatic concerns, it was essential for Gregory to return to Zimbabwe immediately. One could surmise only that, while the president may have been speaking from his heart in the morning, he had probably done so without first ascertaining what his own State Department's position was.

In subsequent days and weeks, Bob continued to maintain daily phone contact with key figures in Washington. Now that the politicians were involved, his task was to help sustain their interest and to enlist further support as needed. By the end of the first week in January, Gregory's cause was no longer just Bob's cause or my cause or Legal Aid's cause. It was now unwaveringly espoused by the likes of senators Moynihan and Helms. State Department functionaries might have been able to ignore the pleas of the Legal Aid Society in December, but the upper-echelons of the State Department and, indeed, the Reagan administration could not simply ignore esteemed members of the Senate Foreign Relations Committee. This same committee is involved in conducting hearings and making recommendations regarding administration appointments, legislation concerning foreign affairs, and the appropriation of funds for various programs.

No, the State Department did not necessarily have absolute power in this matter, as had been suggested by the history of the case thus far. The power and influence of the legislative branch of government still had to be reckoned with. The concept of checks and balances via the separation of powers in our federal government was beginning to come into play.

14. Let's Take It To a Higher Court

THURSDAY, JANUARY 7, 1988, was a cold, crisp, wintry day in New York. Bob McMahon, Tom Ring, Joe Carrieri, and I met for breakfast at a Howard Johnson's Restaurant in Roslyn, New York, and drove to lower Manhattan in Joe's car. Our destination was the United States Court of Appeals for the Second Circuit.

The appeals court was set to hear arguments on the appeal of Judge Weinstein's orders granting physical custody of Gregory to the government and on his injunction preventing all state courts from proceeding in any appeals at the state level. The appellant's brief had been prepared by Lenore Gittis and the staff of the Legal Aid Society as attorney for the plaintiff, Gregory. Joe was going to participate as counsel for the guardian *ad litem*, Bob. Tom and I went along to provide any background information as needed, and to be available for questions from the media, if necessary.

We arrived to an almost carnival atmosphere in the lobby outside the courtroom. There were numerous government officials, including some familiar faces from Monday's hearing at the district court. There were representatives and attorneys for New York City's Special Services for Children and the Legal Aid Society. State Department representatives were standing off to one side with two officials from the Zimbabwean government. There were media everywhere! Press cards were being flashed as impromptu interviews were being conducted with whomever the press could grab. Every aspect of the media was represented, from local and national television and radio to local and national newspapers and magazines.

Inside the courtroom, the atmosphere was electric. The gallery was overflowing with spectators and the media. I took a seat next to WNBC-TV reporter Bob Teague, whose work I had admired for two decades. Bob McMahon sat behind me, next to an NBC News producer, while Tom Ring took a seat next to Corporation Counsel Bob Wayburn. Joe sat among the Legal Aid Society group at the appellant's table, facing the enormous elevated bench that extended some twenty feet from side to side. The courtroom fell silent as the three-judge panel entered. In came The Honorable Ralph K. Winter, Frank X. Altimari, and Ellsworth A. Van Graafeiland.

Henry Weintraub began the arguments for the appeal. Throughout the entire proceedings I was very much impressed by the highly professional and relentless manner in which he and his colleagues carried themselves. These were not high-priced corporate lawyers going through the motions of building a financially successful career. No, they were there as champions of the individual fighting for his rights. Their motives were governed by what they perceived to be justice, fairness, and the protection of the individual. Their kind of efforts contribute mightily to what makes our country so special. In this instance, however, Weintraub was thrown off guard by Judge Winter. Before being able to get fully into the particulars of the case, he was interrupted by the judge, a heavyset, balding man with a ruddy complexion. The judge raised one legal question after another, undercutting the notion that the case should have even been heard. Cases involving diplomatic immunity just didn't have any place in local or federal courts of law, according to Judge Winter. Weintraub tried in vain to keep up with the judge's legal barrage, but he was no match. He'd been forced to depart from his planned approach, and tried unsuccessfully to make impromptu adjustments to the legal arguments. Back in my seat, I felt a letdown. Thus far, the real issues concerning Gregory's safety were not being aired before this vast array of media representatives with their considerable potential for influencing public opinion. So far, it was "The Judge Winter Show."

Following some remarks from Igou Allbray for the government, Joe Carrieri was given a chance to speak in behalf of the guardian *ad litem*. This was to be Joe's first appearance before a U.S. Court of Appeals, a level only one step below the U.S. Supreme Court. Now approaching his mid-fifties, Joe enjoyed a long and distinguished career as an attorney specializing in family law, foster care, and adoption. For twenty years, his firm of Carrieri and Lynch had provided yeoman legal services to the rapidly expanding St. Christopher's Home and, later, St. Christopher-Ottilie. Along the way he had published numerous articles on child welfare issues for the law journals, and had published a comprehensive book on foster care and the law. His most intriguing literary work, however, had absolutely nothing to do with the law or with foster care. It was entitled *Yankee Batboy*.

Joe Carrieri had been the batboy for the New York Yankees throughout their glory years in the 1950s, when they won eight pennants and six world championships in ten years. He had succeeded his brother, who had been the batboy during the 1940s. No one can account for each and every experience that goes into the molding of one's personality. Certainly, genetics play a part in dispositional traits that can be observed early in an infant's life. But there are certain events or circumstances that can't help but leave a lasting impression on the developing personality or character. Once personality characteristics are set, they continue to influence a person's approach to life thereafter. Joe's formative years as an infant, pre-schooler, and schoolboy notwithstanding, those years at Yankee Stadium had to have made a significant contribution to Joe's approach to problems, obstacles, and challenges. Regardless of whatever came before 1950, Joe had been treated to an exciting decade-long course on how to win, how to transform defeat into victory, and how to proceed in the face of seemingly insurmountable odds—and how to refuse to give up.

Joe stood tall and erect. Before he even uttered a word, his body language was communicating an extremely important message: he would not be intimidated. Rather than continue the debate on the law, Joe wisely focused on the facts of the case. He injected the very real human element into the proceedings as he described how terrified was this brutally tortured plaintiff named Gregory. He conjectured about the probable consequences of the stay being lifted.

"The United States government and the Zimbabwean government would have a little boy's form and body, but not his soul or his spirit."

Whenever any of the judges attempted to redirect the focus back to the debate on the law, Joe stormed back, reminding them of their obligations as compassionate human beings.

"You *must not* let this child suffer any more. . . . He *must* be allowed to stay. . . ."

Joe's voice mirrored his words. He introduced passion into that courtroom, and no one sitting there could have possibly remained unmoved. Even if he failed to sufficiently impress all three judges with the merits of overturning Judge Weinstein's order, he must certainly have caught the eyes, ears, and hearts of the many television, radio, newspaper, and magazine reporters who were present in the courtroom. When Joe was finished, I felt like getting up and cheering.

Of the three judges, only one was openly sympathetic to the arguments in behalf of Gregory. Judge Ellsworth Van Graafeiland, probably the eldest of the three, had remained quiet during the first part of the proceeding. When he finally spoke, he could not contain his disdain for and criticism of how the system was operating in a manner that was depriving a little boy of his rights. He was clearly disinterested in the political or international ramifications that supporting Gregory might have. When the point was raised that Zimbabwe might retaliate if we failed to honor the diplomatic immunity of its mission staff, the judge derisively mispronounced the country's name, stating that he didn't care what they thought. No, his priority was clearly with protecting the child rather than with preserving our country's relationship with Zimbabwe.

Later in the afternoon, the court ruled 2–1 "that the order directing that the status quo regarding the child be maintained pending the appeal will be vacated as of 12:00 noon, Saturday, January 9, 1988." Thus, Gregory was again ordered into the physical custody of the State Department. The dissenting opinion was offered by Judge

77

Van Graafeiland, who raised some interesting points, which, to my knowledge, have never been formally answered.

First, Judge Van Graafeiland asked whether the question of diplomatic immunity had been "properly presented and thoroughly explored." He cited the Vienna Convention on Diplomatic Relations:

> When the functions of a person enjoying privileges and immunities have come to an end, such privileges and immunities shall normally cease at the moment when he leaves the country, or on expiry of a reasonable period in which to do so.

When Gregory's father was expelled from the United States on December 21, 1987, were his diplomatic rights terminated at that moment, or did the government "have the right to extend the period of immunity beyond the departure night"? This question of residual diplomatic immunity needed to be addressed before accepting the notion that the conventions of diplomatic immunity applied to Gregory.

Secondly, Judge Van Graafeiland observed:

> Even assuming the argument that diplomatic immunity can be imposed willy-nilly on the infant plaintiff, I am unable to understand how the district court can assume to exercise jurisdiction over the infant as it has done. By what right does the district court order the State Department to take custody of Gregory?

The judge thus raised the possibility that not even the federal courts had jurisdiction in ruling for or against the enforcement of diplomatic immunity laws. This jurisdictional question had bounced from court to court ever since the case was first heard in Queens family court. If the Queens family court did not have jurisdiction over the child of a diplomat, then perhaps the New York state courts or the state Court of Appeals had jurisdiction. If they didn't have jurisdiction, then perhaps the District Court for the

Eastern District did. Judge Weinstein had proceeded as if his court did in fact have jurisdiction in the case when he ordered the State Department to take physical custody of Gregory. Judge Van Graafeiland was now questioning whether the district court or even the U.S. Court of Appeals had a right to rule on Gregory. It is interesting that by raising the question of jurisdiction at the federal court level, the judge was actually agreeing with a position taken by the State Department in a related manner. The State Department had argued on Tuesday, January 5, at a conference concerning the appointment of a guardian *ad litem*, that "because of Gregory's diplomatic status, the [federal district] court lacked jurisdiction to appoint a guardian *ad litem*." In retrospect, it seemed like the State Department wanted to have its cake and eat it at the same time. It wanted the federal courts to rule in favor of granting physical custody, but then argued that federal courts could not interfere by appointing a guardian *ad litem* because the court lacked jurisdiction in the case.

Judge Van Graafeiland concluded his dissenting opinion with the following recommendation:

> In my opinion, this matter should be remanded to the district court for a hearing on the facts and the law as to whether Gregory and/or his parents are covered by diplomatic immunity that cannot be waived, and if the answer to this question is in the affirmative, whether the district court has jurisdiction to enter any order respecting the infant plaintiff.

The judge's opinion was but another moral victory within a succession of a growing number of legal defeats. What awaited us outside the courtroom, however, would prove to be of equal importance to anything that happened inside.

15. The Media Blitz

W HEN BOB, JOE, TOM, and I slowly descended the many steps of the U.S. Court of Appeals building, a phalanx of news reporters, cameras, and microphones were waiting. Reporters clustered around Igou Allbray saw us coming and swarmed in our direction. Minutes earlier, we had agreed to stick close together so that we could present a clear, consistent message, covering and answering any legal, administrative, child care, or clinical question that might arise. The barrage of questions began.

"What specific abuse did the child receive?"

"What are the dangers of moving him?"

"Where is he now? How is he?"

"Won't this lead to Zimbabwe's taking the children of our diplomats?"

"Will you take this to the Supreme Court?"

While this was going on, WNBC-TV reporter Bob Teague, with whom I had sat during the appeal hearing, yanked at my coat to do a separate interview for him. I motioned for him to wait a minute until the group interview was completed, but he was interested in getting his own story, and he yanked more forcefully. Bob McMahon, on the other side of me, noted what was transpiring and held me on my other arm. For a few seconds, I thought I was about to be the subject of a TV tug-of-war, with me playing the part of the rope.

Just like that, the case was a major news story with national media coverage. Remember, just three days earlier the story had been limited to local newspaper coverage pertaining to the succession of court proceedings starting in mid-December. Any conversations between Bob and local newspaper reporters prior to January 4 had been on an anonymous basis and only for the purpose of providing some background information. During the latter part of December and into the first few days of January, Bob did a marvelous job of keeping the local papers interested in the case, thus gradually building up public interest. Following my first appearance on the Fox-TV interview on Monday, the interest of the media progressed geometrically, reaching its zenith on Thursday and Friday.

On Tuesday, I taped an interview for "NBC Nightly News," which was not aired. The producer did not feel that the segment could be used without also having a picture of Gregory so that viewers could better identify with the subject of the story. At the end of that interview, I addressed the government and people of Zimbabwe, asking for their assistance in resolving one little boy's problem. Unfortunately, that message never got beyond 30 Rockefeller Center.

On Wednesday, a remote crew from "Eyewitness News" interviewed me in my office in Jamaica, mixing up my name with that of former Miami Dolphins quarterback Bob Griese. That segment included an interview with Gary Kipling, shot from behind. The reason for this, given by the reporter, was that "the foster father feared for his own safety," which was totally inaccurate. As much as we appreciated the assistance of the media in disseminating Gregory's story and generating public support, there was also a growing caution about the dangers of being exploited and having the truth distorted.

The pressure for an interview with or a picture of Gregory mounted feverishly. There were calls from "60 Minutes," "World News Tonight," and "The McNeil-Lehrer Report," to name but a few. Our primary concern, however, was for Gregory's safety and privacy. He was a frightened child who had finally found a safe haven where he could shut out the menacing, threatening life that he had led to that point. He did not wish to be seen or to have his whereabouts discovered, lest somehow such discovery would lead to his being returned to his father. Furthermore, the very unpredictable factors involved in subjecting Gregory to news people, who, though well-meaning, may very well have followed misguided instincts in questioning Gregory, put his direct exposure to the media out of the question.

Some news people proved themselves to be extremely understanding and humane in their treatment of the story. One in particular was Fox-TV's Bob O'Brien. We first met O'Brien while waiting for the decision of the U.S. Court of Appeals at the courthouse late Thursday afternoon. He listened intently as we described the horrors that Gregory was exposed to and the paralyzing terror that he now felt regarding being sent back to his father. With each detail, O'Brien's face became a little redder and angrier. As a father himself, he was obviously a person who could feel for and identify with the child, responding to Gregory's misfortunes as if they had happened to his own child. When the decision was handed out, our hearts sank collectively, but no one was more visibly shaken and outraged than was O'Brien. "Oh my God! How can they do this? This is terrible!" he exclaimed.

He was genuinely touched. He declared he was prepared to go to Washington or even to Zimbabwe to see that this miscarriage of justice was corrected. Most significant, however, was that he was prepared to suppress his reportorial instincts and responsibilities in the interests of following the guidelines of those who were responsible for Gregory's welfare. He could be entrusted with information not intended for broadcast, despite the opportunity for the media's universal lust for a scoop. Throughout the entire period, O'Brien's sustained interest and sensitive handling of Gregory's story reached the highest professional journalistic standard, for which all of us were most grateful. In fact, O'Brien was to become Gregory's favorite newsman, to the extent that he later came to refer to himself alternatively as "Gregory O'Brien" or "Bob O'Gregory" when he interviewed others with our video camera.

Through the middle of January, Gregory was shielded from television and newspaper reports of his case, out of concern for resensitizing him to fears over the growing prospects of being returned to

Zimbabwe. One evening, however, he was watching a movie on television with Jeremy and Adam Kipling. During a commercial break there was a brief preview from the newsroom about the lead story for the ten o'clock news: Gregory's court battle. When Gregory heard his name he shrieked and ran to get Gary, who was in another room. Gary tried to discourage Gregory from staying up to see the news, but Gregory insisted.

"It's my life they're talking about. I have to see it!"

That was the first time he ever saw Bob O'Brien, and it left a lasting, positive impression on him. The realization that others cared about his plight was a therapeutic tonic to a child who had felt so alone for such a long time.

During the twenty-four hours following the appeals court decision, the phones were ringing off the hook at Bob's office in Sea Cliff, at Joe's office in Jericho, and at my office in Jamaica. Calls from reporters from coast to coast were received, representing such papers as the *Los Angeles Times, Chicago Tribune, Boston Globe, Washington Post,* and *USA Today.* All wanted to know our reaction to the loss in court and whether the case would be going to the Supreme Court. I began to sympathize with public officials who are forced to repeat answers or statements over and over again for various interviews or speeches. Of all my comments throughout the five-day period of January 4 through 8, none captured my mood and position better than those made for CBS radio in the early evening of January 7, after the appeals court defeat. My sense of outrage and disillusionment with a system of justice that was too impotent to protect a defenseless nine-year-old boy were expressed in these words:

> We're standing on the steps of the federal courthouse, and Gregory is *screaming* for help. But all he hears in return is silence; silence from the family court, silence from the state courts, silence from the federal courts—not because the courts do not care, but because no one seems to have juris-diction in safeguarding this child's human rights.

Saying these words gave me a good feeling. Hearing them on my car radio as I drove to work the next morning engendered an even greater sense of pride in what we were striving to accomplish. The experience of Thursday invigorated me to push forward with more energy than ever. With New York being hit with a major snowstorm, most of my Friday clients canceled. It gave me some time to gather my thoughts and to derive some meaning from the events of recent days, particularly pertaining to the frustrating legal battle that we were losing. I began to write down my thoughts, and by mid-afternoon I had completed the following essay, "Is There a Court for Human Rights?"

As I sat in the courtroom of the United States Court of Appeals for the Second Circuit on January 7, listening to arguments for and against the immediate, forcible return of nine-year-old Gregory Tanaka to Zimbabwe, I was perplexed. All parties appeared to show genuine concern for the child, yet it became increasingly clear that his best interests were not being served. The complexity of the case deserves much but not all the blame for this reality. At stake were multiple issues involving various levels of our legal system, international diplomacy, and an individual's human rights. The most promising outcome would have been a decision that somehow could have been equally satisfactory from a legal, diplomatic, and humanitarian perspective. As this was apparently not possible, priorities were set, and human rights finished last!

Gregory, the victim of severe and chronic physical and psychological abuse by his father, is a child of at least average intelligence who has consistently and clearly articulated his opposition to being removed from his foster home (where he has been for the past month) at the present time. The risks of sending him home precipitously have been described and documented throughout the legal proceedings, which have included arguments in family court, N.Y. state court, N.Y. state Court of Appeals, U.S. District Court for the Eastern District of New York, and U.S. Court of Appeals for the Second Circuit: "He appears prone to responding by withdrawing in whatever way necessary from what he considers would be a tremendously threatening situation. . . . Gregory's last resort would be to break from reality through decompensation manifested by a total regressive reaction. The last alternative would most certainly require some form of hospitalization or institutionalization with guarded prognosis at best." Such eventuality appears likely if Gregory were to be immediately transferred to live with anyone whom he perceives to be associated with Zimbabwe. He vehemently contends that, in view of his father's prominent status within the Zimbabwean community, he would be promptly returned to his father's care and would be subjected to a resumption of the same physical and psychological torture as before. It is Gregory's present perception that a return to any Zimbabwean family is tantamount to a return to his father. By subjecting him to a situation which for him would be terrifying over a prolonged period of time, he would be receiving a form of psychological torture that would jeopardize his already tenuous emotional well-being.

In one dissenting vote on Thursday, Circuit Judge Ellsworth A. Van Graafeiland observed: "Where the health and the welfare of a nine-year-old child is concerned, I believe that we should proceed with extreme care. I do not believe we are doing that in this case." This is precisely the position taken by St. Christopher-Ottilie, Services for Children and Families, which is the foster care agency involved. The primary objective in any foster care placement is to explore any and all possibilities for a rehabilitation of the total or partial family unit. Working through and resolving individual and family issues, concerns, conflicts, and fears is best accomplished in an atmosphere of security and trust. Gregory urgently needs sufficient time to learn to trust again and to deal with the emotional and physical scars he has endured. Parallel to individual therapy, parental counseling for his mother and, ultimately, family therapy would be crucial components of an effective treatment plan. Such approach has been applied successfully in the past in other cases involving physical and psychological abuse. It is anticipated that, along with incontrovertible proof that Gregory's safety would not be jeopardized by his father upon the boy's return to Zimbabwe, such a treatment plan could accomplish its objectives within the relatively brief period of a few months.

At the outset I stated that not all of the blame for Gregory's cloudy and threatened future lies with the complexity of the case. The balance of the blame may be attributed to a small, yet significant crack in our two hundred-year-old Constitution. Despite our role as a world leader, championing the fight for human rights from Russia to South Africa, there appears to be no court in our own country whose jurisdiction covers actual or potential violations of human rights. Clearly, many of the human rights set forth in the 1948 U.N. Universal Declaration of Human Rights are being or may be denied Gregory, simply because he's a child and happens to be the son of a government official who formerly enjoyed diplomatic immunity. Gregory ironically enjoys fewer rights as a human being because of the special "protections" imposed upon him as the son of a diplomat. Which of the human rights are being withheld? Article 3: ". . . the right to life, liberty, and the security of person"; Article 5: "No one shall be subjected to torture or to cruel, inhuman or degrading treatment or punishment"; Article 7: "All are equal before the law and are entitled without any discrimination to equal protection of the law"; Article 9: "No one shall be subjected to arbitrary arrest, detention, or exile"; Article 14: "Everyone has the right to seek and to enjoy in other countries asylum from persecution."

Gregory has just about run out of legal options. He is pleading his case loudly and clearly, yet no one has the "jurisdiction" to help him. It seems to me that the Court for Human Rights, although not stipulated in our constitution, must be called into action. It is the humanitarian voice of the people of America and the world that must respond.

I had intended to submit the essay to the *New York Times* for its OpEd page, but it was neither sent nor published. Late in the afternoon, I received a phone call from Bob, who wanted to bring me up to date on a few developments. One development was that the Legal Aid Society had sent Elizabeth Johanns to Washington, D.C., to file an appeal with the Supreme Court.

A second development concerned a request from State Department. The caller had stated that the State Department wished to work with us cooperatively in resolving the problem of returning Gregory to Zimbabwe when he was ready to go. No specifics regarding a time frame or a definition of what was meant by "ready" were given. Yet this message introduced a glimmer of hope in what had become an extremely bleak picture. One stipulation was added. The caller requested and received our agreement to a news blackout. Speaking in behalf of the St. Christopher-Ottilie people, Bob agreed to say nothing further to the press. It was evident that the considerable media exposure of the past few days had registered significantly at the higher levels of the State Department. Sensitivity about negative publicity, and concern about minimizing the public outcry in behalf of keeping Gregory in the U.S. seemed to dictate the State Department's altered posture.

January 8 marked the beginning of a new relationship with the State Department—or so we hoped. There was no way of knowing for sure what the true intentions of the government were, but by then there seemed little to lose in acquiescing to the State Department's request. My essay was safely filed away.

16. The Supreme Court Decides

I N ITS DECISION to lift the stay of the order for Gregory to be placed in the custody of the State Department, the United States Court of Appeals for the Second Circuit set twelve noon on Saturday, January 9, as the new deadline.

Following the appellate decision on Thursday, a brief meeting was held at Legal Aid Society offices in lower Manhattan to determine what steps to take next. All of the Legal Aid and St. Christopher-Ottilie staffs who had attended the Court of Appeals proceedings earlier in the day were present.

It appeared that Legal Aid was a bit miffed about the contradictory position taken by Joe Carrieri, compared with that of Henry Weintraub. While Henry had adhered to the legal arguments supporting Gregory's right to due process in his asylum petition, Joe had focused on the human issue of how best to protect a terrified little boy from further, more debilitating psychological trauma. Joe had wittingly downplayed the need or desire for permanent asylum, which may have been a source of embarrassment for the Legal Aid people.

At one point in our deliberations that Thursday evening, Weintraub asked, "What does Gregory want? Does he want asylum? Does he want to be an American?"

"He doesn't want to be an American," I responded. "He wants to be safe. He has a bond with his mother that he does not wish to sever."

Despite the apparent inconsistency between the direction of the legal battle and the clinical objectives for Gregory, it was agreed by all that taking the case the last mile—to the U.S. Supreme Court—was still advisable. Essentially, although there was little hope of having a reversal in the Court, the action would buy some more time for a miracle to happen. Perhaps the miracle would come in the form of an irrefutable public outcry in behalf of Gregory, making the State Department reconsider its modus operandi in securing his physical custody.

On Friday, January 8, the Legal Aid Society, in the person of Elizabeth Johanns, filed an application with Justice Thurgood Marshall of the U.S. Supreme Court for a stay of the January 4 orders of Judge Weinstein. The orders were stayed by Justice Harry Blackmun pending completion of *certiorari* proceedings in the Court. It would be a full week before the Court would finally announce its decision.

On January 16, the *Los Angeles Times* reported that on Friday, January 15, "the U.S. Supreme Court bowed to the demands of international law and politics and ordered that the boy be returned to the custody of his family." The *Chicago Tribune* explained that "the Court lifted the stay Friday in a closed-door conference, and announced its decision without comment. None of the justices recorded a dissent."

The decision and press reports were widely interpreted by the public to mean that Gregory was to be immediately carted off to Zimbabwe. In our country, most of us are conditioned to believe that the Supreme Court is there to give the final word, beyond which there is absolutely no recourse. Thus, when headlines read "Boy's Return to Zimbabwe Ordered by Supreme Court," many believed it was a foregone conclusion that Gregory would be on the next plane to Africa. The legal battle was over. Joe Carrieri later wrote:

> I was horrified that every court involved in Gregory's problem, which included the family court, the appellate division, the state Court of Appeals, the eastern and southern districts of the federal court, the Court of Appeals for

the Second Circuit, and the Supreme Court of the United States, all loudly and clearly promulgated the doctrine that diplomatic immunity was not only a shield against prosecution, but it was a sword preventing the system from helping Gregory, who was used and abused but never abandoned.

Despite the loss in the Supreme Court, Gregory was not seized and placed on the next plane out. On the contrary, by the date of the Supreme Court decision, it was becoming increasingly clear that, although we had lost the battle in the courts, we were winning the war over protecting Gregory from further psychological harm. In its brief to the Supreme Court, the State Department had as much as guaranteed that Gregory's emotional condition would be of paramount importance in determining when he could be transferred.

> The government is taking steps to ensure that any transfer of physical custody of Gregory preceding his return to Zimbabwe is effected in such a way as to minimize trauma to the child. . . . The Department of State is consulting closely with Dr. Heacock and working with the St. Christopher-Ottilie organization as well as the Zimbabwean mission to ensure that the transfer of physical custody takes place in a medically sound manner. The immediate objective is to reduce the psychological stress on Gregory that derives from his mistaken belief that he will not be protected from his father if he leaves his current environment and returns to Zimbabwe. The Department of State has not yet determined precisely how long it will take to prepare Gregory for the transfer.

I couldn't have written the above any better if my intention had been to promote St. Christopher-Ottilie rather than the State Department position. In fact, our positions had practically merged into one. Charles Redman, a State Department spokesman, responded to a question concerning the timetable for Gregory's transfer: "It may be a long process rather than a short one."

Mazel tov! The Department of State was now espousing our position. It had gone on record in the media and with the Supreme Court as promising to do everything necessary to safeguard Gregory's emotional condition in the process of transferring him to his homeland. Unfortunately, by this time there was little trust placed in the statements coming from the State Department. The media and the public and, to some extent, some of us at St. Christopher-Ottilie remained skeptical of the government's newly stated resolve to protect Gregory. After all, weren't these the same people who sent a U.S. marshal to Gary Kipling's home on January 4 in preparation for dragging Gregory out, kicking and screaming? Only time and action would reveal what the government's true intentions really were.

In the meantime, an air of skepticism and cynicism about the government's motives prevailed in the press. A January 25 WNBC-TV editorial lambasted our government for preparing to "sacrifice an innocent, helpless child on the altar of diplomatic expediency."

A similar sentiment was voiced in a *Wall Street Journal* editorial the following day: "There is no justification for Gregory Tanaka's chances for a happy childhood to be sacrificed on an altar of diplomacy."

17. Back to Basics:
Case Planning for Foster Care

E VEN BEFORE it became evident that the State Department might work with us and give sufficient time to effect a therapeutic transfer, we decided to start functioning as though we were definitely going to have that time. From mid-December through the first week of January, Gregory's status changed on a daily, and sometimes hourly basis. Everything was so unpredictable and beyond our control that any thought of effective case planning was deferred. How could a case plan or treatment plan be developed or implemented when no one knew whether Gregory would be with us from one day to the next?

Nevertheless, as the case headed for the U.S. Court of Appeals and the U.S. Supreme Court, it behooved us to initiate a responsible plan, including whatever social services and clinical services were necessary. After walking on eggshells for weeks, it was time to get down to basics, to standard operating procedures that are applied when any child enters foster care. In any placement, one never knows when an unforeseen event will result in the abrupt, untimely discharge of a child before a treatment plan for him or her and the natural family can be successfully completed. Despite the possibility of such a surprise eventuality, it is still incumbent upon the responsible agency and its treatment team to proceed with the established treatment plan for as long as feasible.

On Wednesday, January 6, one day before the Court of Appeals action, Bob McMahon formally convened the members of

Gregory's treatment team for the purpose of establishing a case plan. The team consisted of Yara Fernandez, who was functioning as Gregory's caseworker in the absence of Stephanie Rothstein; Tom Ring, who was functioning as the casework supervisor; Gary Kipling, serving in the role of Gregory's foster parent; and myself, as Gregory's psychologist and prospective therapist. Bob, who had just been appointed Gregory's guardian *ad litem* the day before, chaired the meeting at his Sea Cliff office. For the first time in two weeks, we were engaging in a familiar activity that was routine in our field. We were able briefly to suspend any considerations of how this or that judge might rule, or what the State Department might require.

Within a forty-minute period, a simple, focused plan was devised "to ensure the child's emotional, physical, and mental well-being." The case objective was for Gregory to achieve a level of functioning that would permit a reconciliation with his family. Gregory's clinical, educational, medical, recreational, and religious needs were spelled out. In the clinical area, twice-weekly individual psychotherapy sessions were prescribed with the following goal:

> Gregory will learn to trust again and to deal with the emotional and physical scars he has endured. . . . Optimally, the psychotherapy treatment will progress to the level that it will include parental counseling and ultimately family therapy.

Provisions for visitations between Gregory and his mother and sisters were incorporated into the plan as well. It was emphasized that such "visits are seen as key to the implementation of the service plan." In such simple, straightforward, and traditional terms was our general approach to this extraordinary case proclaimed. Of course, the complexities of the case promised to make implementation of the plan challenging, to say the least, but we were now back to doing what we knew best.

18. The Therapy Mission:
Treatment for an Abused Child

THE EVENING OF Saturday, January 9, found my wife, Susanne, my middle son, Adam, and myself driving to the Copacabana in Manhattan to attend a lavish bar mitzvah celebration for one of Adam's friends. All decked out in formal attire, I was especially looking forward to a respite from the frantic, non-stop pressures of the previous two weeks. The car radio was on when suddenly a familiar voice was heard. It was Bob McMahon being interviewed for perhaps the last time prior to the news blackout we had agreed to honor. Bob was being asked the standard questions of the day concerning his reactions to the latest developments and Gregory's up-to-the-minute status. He used the opportunity to announce: "Gregory has begun to receive psychotherapeutic treatment from Dr. Leonard Gries, our director of Mental Health Services. We are hopeful that such treatment will help him to build the trust necessary for him to eventually return to his homeland."

If anyone was apprehensive at the moment, it was I. I felt a rush of anxiety as I contemplated the import of what Bob was saying. The responsibility of affecting a significant and fairly rapid change in Gregory's emotional state was being publicly laid on my shoulders. The treatment process that was to bring about such change was to occur under considerable public scrutiny. Even under normal conditions, there are many variables that may delay the attainment of treatment goals. In this case, there were countless obstacles that promised to make the course of therapy less than predictable.

I had a sobering thought as we stood in front of the Copa. "What if Gregory doesn't respond to treatment?"

I quickly reassured myself by recalling how other abused children responded favorably to treatment. It was imperative that I apply a similar approach in working with Gregory.

Gregory required what other child abuse victims require. This might best be appreciated if the components of the child abuse syndrome are first understood. Aside from the physical harm that is incurred, the psychological harm to a chronically abused child often lasts a lifetime. When we are infants and young children, our views of others, of our environment, and of ourselves are molded by our experiences and relationships with our parents. Whether we are trusting of others derives from our trust or mistrust of our parents. Whether we see our environment as orderly, benevolent, and loving derives from the lessons we learn from our prototypical relationship with our parents. Whether or not we see ourselves as lovable, worthy, valued individuals derives from the messages of love and worth that may or may not be present in our parents' interactions with us. The abused child is not only the victim of physical battering, he is also usually the victim of a chronic defect within the child-rearing environment. He feels worthless and unloved—how can someone who is valued highly and loved be treated in such a disdainful manner? He feels powerless to do anything about his mistreatment. He is practically incapable of trusting anyone, particularly adults. To compensate for feelings of powerlessness and mistrust, he has an intense need to control and manipulate others. To compensate for feelings of weakness, he tends to act aggressively, if not violently, toward his peers. His emotional need for love and affection translates behaviorally into a need for immediate gratification and high impulsivity.

Beneath this angry, controlling, impulsive behavioral veneer, however, is a depressed, lonely, and fearful youngster, utterly convinced of his worthlessness. At some level, most if not all abused children believe that it is their own culpability, their own badness that justified the harsh, abusive treatment received at the hands of their parent or parents. Rather than accept the notion of having a malevolent parent, the abused child typically denies this reality and displaces the quality of malevolence onto himself. He splits his views of people and himself into either all good or all bad. The typical abused child winds up with an all-bad representation of himself. He defends against such a negative self-image as well as against the overwhelming threat of annihilation in a number of ways. At a basic level, he engages in physical and/or emotional distancing. He avoids contact with and proximity to people while remaining exceedingly wary and hyper-vigilant. Simultaneously, he shuts off as much of his emotional life as possible, as manifested by a bland, constricted affect, seemingly unmoved or unperturbed by anything—even another beating.

When such defense fails to ward off the deep feelings of anxiety and rage associated with past, then beatings, memories, and feelings related to the original traumas begin to permeate the child's life, in his play, fantasies, and dreams. In his interactions with others he unwittingly recreates the abusive relationship either by playing in the role of the abused or by identifying with the aggressor parent in the role of the abuser. In either case, his relationships with others continue to suffer, thereby reinforcing his image of himself as a bad person. It gets to be like a broken record as the child repeatedly falls back into the cycle of feeling worthless, followed by acting in an inappropriate manner to provoke attention, followed by adult abusive and/or rejecting behavior, followed by intensified feelings of worthlessness. Psychologically, the child is futilely attempting to master a painful emotional situation by repeating it thematically, over and over again. Things get worse, not better.

At the core of the abused child's inability to correct his dysfunctional relationships is a poorly functioning ego. Because of his developmental history of being raised within a malevolent rather than protective parental environment, the child fails to learn effective ways of coping and caring for himself. He is less likely to be able to handle problems in an effective, reality-based manner. Such a defect in functioning often extends into social and educational spheres, resulting in academic and conduct difficulties at school.

Without treatment, the abused child is likely to repeat the abusive trauma in one form or another as he grows older. With the passage of time, the probability that the child will grow into an assaultive, homicidal, or suicidal adult is increased. Failure at school and work and as a parent is likely as well. The tragic irony is that the untreated abused child is most apt to copy the parenting style to which he was subjected while growing up, and will wind up being an abusive parent himself. This bleak scenario can be prevented by timely intervention, including providing immediate relief to the child via ensuring a safe environment, providing individual psychotherapy for him and parental counseling for the parents (both the abusing and nonabusing parent), leading to family therapy. Depending on the case, special educational intervention may be needed for the child and individual psychotherapy may be needed for one or both parents. Usually, one or two years of such a total treatment package is necessary in order to attain durable gains for the child and the family.

In Gregory's case, we were working with two strikes against us. The international pressure to have him returned to Zimbabwe created a tremendous time pressure. Instead of two years, we would be lucky if we were given two months within which to affect significant change. Secondly, the inaccessibility to the rest of his family created a severe handicap. Gregory's father was seven thousand miles away and his mother was insulated from us by the Zimbabwean government. How could we then get a comprehensive history of the child or the parent-child conflicts? How could we begin to counsel even one of the parents on methods of rebuilding trust and communication with Gregory? How could we effectively prepare Gregory for transfer to a supposedly safe environment that was unknown to us?

Since we didn't have answers to these questions, the only thing for us to do was adapt to the situation as it existed. Treatment objectives had to be tailored to what could be accomplished within the relatively short period of two to three months, and so must be somewhat limited in scope. I didn't dare even to fantasize that within such a brief period of time Gregory could be living safely and happily with his parents at their home in Zimbabwe. I did feel it was quite possible, however, that he could be living in a foster care setting in Zimbabwe by then, and at least be engaged in the early phases of attempting to restore positive relationships with his mother and sisters.

On Sunday, January 10, I met again with Dr. Heacock to discuss a treatment plan. Fortunately, we were in agreement on a diagnostic formulation of Gregory's condition as well as on what approach should be taken in treatment. We agreed that individual treatment should focus on helping Gregory find appropriate expression of his rage and fear, helping him develop and master adaptive coping skills to assist in his efforts to gain adult attention and to feel more in control. In addition, Gregory would eventually need to understand his own role in eliciting his father's abusive behavior. It was agreed that I would be responsible for conducting the individual therapy sessions with Gregory, while Dr. Heacock would attempt to engage Gregory's mother to begin the parental counseling process. We were eager to initiate innocuous visits between Gregory and his mother.

I completed the proposed treatment plan on January 11. The plan is reproduced here verbatim:

TREATMENT PLAN
Re: Gregory Tanaka
1/11/88

TREATMENT GOAL I:
Prepare child for returning to mother, if feasible, while ensuring his emotional and physical well-being.
- *Treatment Objectives I:*
1. Develop therapeutic relationship which will foster the rebuilding of trust in significant others (e.g., mother).
    a. Develop schemas for determining when and whom to trust.
2. Identify and ventilate feelings of rage and fear vis-à-vis family members.
3. Clarify reasons and circumstances surrounding father's abusive treatment and mother's failure to protect.
    a. Explore child's role in provoking abusive incidents.
4. Develop adaptive coping skills to replace more rigid and extreme defenses that have been utilized by child as a means to assert control.

5. Establish positive body image, self-identity, and feeling of wholeness to counteract damaged identity associated with body scars and memories of past traumatic events.

• *Treatment Approach I:*
Gregory will be seen for short-term, individual psychotherapy, addressing each of the above objectives. Twice weekly, 50-minute therapy sessions will be conducted by Dr. Leonard Gries at the Jamaica office of St. Christopher-Ottilie. Progress in treatment will be communicated to Dr. Donald Heacock, who will interview the child in conjunction with family visits with regard to his readiness for transfer.

TREATMENT GOAL II:
Assist mother in preparing for return of child through the enhancement of her understanding of past family problems and of appropriate child-rearing practices.
• *Treatment Objectives II:*
1. Establish a dialogue with mother.
    a. Secure a full history of family and child.
2. Encourage a resumption of visits between mother and son.
    a. Emphasize nonconfrontational approach to visits.
    b. Develop listening and speaking skills of mother.
3. Clarify mother's understanding and analysis of past family problems, focusing on the abuse in particular.
    a. Clarify mother's position regarding her present and future relationship with her husband.
4. Explore necessary safeguards required by child to enable his development of trust in mother or substitute caretaker.
5. Explore nonrepressive forms of discipline which promote an appreciation by child of the natural and logical consequences of his actions.

• *Treatment Approach II:*
Mrs. Tanaka will be seen for parent counseling on a weekly basis by Dr. Donald Heacock. The sessions, which will last for approximately 50 minutes, will directly precede scheduled

weekly visits between mother and child. The weekly visits will take place at the Jamaica office of St. Christopher-Ottilie, and will be observed and monitored by Dr. Heacock, Dr. Gries, and casework supervisor, Yara Fernandez. Dr. Gries will consult with Dr. Heacock on a weekly basis regarding progress in the parent counseling. Provisions for family therapy, including Gregory's sisters, will be made as warranted by progress in Gregory's individual therapy and parent counseling.

- *Treatment II—Alternative Provisions:*
In the event that Mrs. Tanaka is inaccessible for parent counseling, family therapy, and visitations, then the above plan would be applied to another caretaker designated by the Zimbabwean government. Treatment Objective 4 (i.e., "Explore necessary safeguards required by child to enable his development of trust") would receive the most emphasis. The specifics of what would happen once Gregory returned to Zimbabwe would have to be clearly detailed and presented to him in the context of conjoint sessions. Ideally, the same Zimbabwean caretaker would retain physical custody for a sufficient period of time in Zimbabwe before any other transfer is contemplated. Consideration should be given to identifying a trusted and competent extended family member (e.g., aunt or uncle) who may be designated caretaker here and/or in Zimbabwe.

- *Decisions Regarding Transfer:*
All decisions regarding any change in the above plan, as well as concerning Gregory's readiness for transfer to his mother or another Zimbabwean family, will be reached following full consultation among the treatment team members, who include:

    Dr. Leonard Gries

    Dr. Donald Heacock

    Ms. Yara Fernandez

    Mr. Thomas Ring

Recommendations for change will be made to St. Christopher-Ottilie's executive director, Mr. Bob McMahon, who will consider feasibility in collaboration with State Department officials.

Every effort will be made to expedite this process and to achieve all treatment objectives within a reasonable time frame (i.e., less than four months). Where progress is not evidenced, treatment objectives and/or methods may require revision.

Leonard T. Gries, Ph.D.   Donald Heacock, M.D.
Psychologist   Consulting Psychiatrist
Director, Mental Health Services   U.S. State Department
St. Christopher-Ottilie

Therapy actually started several days prior to the writing of the treatment plan when I met with Gregory on Wednesday, January 6. A treatment plan spells out goals objectively in a nice, orderly fashion, but treatment never proceeds so neatly and predictably. The task of the therapist is to be available to the child and to be ever alert to opportunities for pursuing treatment objectives in whatever way or order they appear during the sessions. The primary task of the therapist is to establish a close, trusting relationship between the child and the therapist. All other objectives hinge upon this establishment of a therapeutic alliance. The considerable mistrust found in the abused child makes this a much more difficult task than is usually the case.

Early in a new relationship, the distrustful child engages in much testing behavior in an effort to determine whether the new person is to be trusted. Gregory did this with the Kiplings, and he did it in our initial therapy sessions as well. Typically, the testing behavior continues and worsens until one of two things happens. The other person may be pushed to the limit of his tolerance, finally reacting in a critical manner, which confirms to the child that this is just another rejection from someone he can't trust. Alternatively, the other person may demonstrate unconditional acceptance of the child while benignly imposing limits on the child's behavior. Once the child sees that he cannot sway the other person against him, he allows himself to begin to trust. This is the essence of what transpires during the initial phase of therapy, particularly when a distrustful child is the client. Feeling truly accepted by an adult imbued with power and authority, as is the therapist in the eyes of the child client, is such an important, potent step in the direction of the child's beginning to accept and to like himself. The process of converting the bad-person self image into a good-person self image thus begins.

During that first session with Gregory, his bad-person image was very evident. He told me he was good at nothing, "except remembering." I used that one area of perceived competence to invite Gregory to talk about his past. His pride in his memory facilitated his willingness to conjure up even memories of Zimbabwe. Surprisingly, by the second session, on January 11, Gregory was referring to pleasant memories from his days in Zimbabwe. In fact, when he was asked to think of the most pleasant scene in his life, he came up with the memory of being with a friend in his home in Zimbabwe at the age of five. I inferred that there must be a storehouse of other pleasant memories of life in Zimbabwe, memories that would begin to assume a more alluring intensity as time away from family passed.

Several other significant themes emerged during the first two therapy sessions. One concerned Gregory's preoccupation with death, which was on his mind much more than was evident. At the conclusion of the first session, Gregory asked, "Do you remember when you are going to die?"

That was Gregory's rather awkward way of introducing his concerns about death to me. I later concluded that this reflected the degree of terror that he was living under on a daily basis. He was continuously terrified of being caught and killed by his father. Fear for Gregory was at a life-or-death level.

The use of metaphor is an indispensable tool for working with children in therapy. It provides clear, abbreviated images symbolizing and clarifying the issues and conflicts that face them. During the second session, Gregory and I were enjoying the board game Trouble, which provided a simple parallel to what Gregory was concerned about most in his life: the danger of being suddenly sent home when he was so close to a permanent safety zone. For Gregory, whose safety zone was now Gary Kipling's home, the specter of being swept away without warning or preparation was central to his fears. In such a situation, all control is in the hands of others, with little if any control remaining with the child. Finding appropriate ways to assert personal control—an important task for any abused child—was certainly vital to Gregory.

We concluded the second session with a discussion of how to go about getting what one wants without angering others or alienating oneself. Gregory explained how he had threatened Joannie Kipling in a prior attempt to blackmail her into reading a bedtime story. He told her that he wouldn't go to sleep or stay in bed unless she told a story. The threat didn't work. I interjected how much I was looking forward to having a steak dinner at home later in the evening, but I expressed uncertainty over how to approach my wife to get her to prepare a steak. Should I call her and demand that she make a steak? Should I threaten her over making the steak? Should I express my needs and wishes in the form of a request? Gregory enjoyed being called in as a consultant in this manner. This "consultant procedure" is an approach I've often used effectively to involve children in issues and questions that are similar to their personal concerns.

The following day, Gary called to give me an update on Gregory. He informed me of Gregory's first experience viewing his story on television the night before. That was the night that he insisted on staying up because it was his life they were talking about. It was most heartening for Gregory to see and hear how so many people—from Bob O'Brien to the members of the Supreme Court to people from Zimbabwe and, most significantly, his mother—were all voicing their concern about him. Gregory went to sleep without a struggle that evening. He asked for and received a brief bedtime story. Before the lights were turned out, he asked Gary to call me to find out: "Did Lenny get his steak dinner tonight?"

Treatment was only two sessions old, but Gregory was certainly tuned right in.

Arthur Green, M.D., an esteemed expert in the psychiatric treatment of abused children, stated in the book *Post-Traumatic Stress Disorders in Children* (edited by S. Eth and R. Pynoos, 1985), "It is therapeutic to allow the child to master the trauma [of being abused] by repetition and symbolic reenactment with dolls, puppets, and drawings." The child can often achieve through play what is so painfully elusive in real life: a successful resolution of his family ordeal.

Resolution may come in many forms. On January 13, at his third session, Gregory was able to fantasize two distinctly different resolutions in his puppet play. Initially, Gregory's solution to a critical, punitive father was to have the father receive the same treatment or worse in return. He hurled the father puppet into the closet with a vengeance. This provided much needed opportunity for a cathartic, safe expression of the tremendous rage that had been accumulating for months and longer. With this accomplished, Gregory resumed the puppet play and eventually formulated a completely different resolution of the father-son conflict. The mother puppet became more active, interceding in the child's behalf, and convinced the father puppet to change his ways and to view the child differently. *Voilà!* Gregory was offering in fantasy his desired resolution of his terrible family ordeal. Somehow he felt he would have to rely upon his mother's support and intervention in his behalf—something that hadn't occurred in the past.

That Gregory's mother was weighing more and more on his mind was confirmed later in the third session, when he acknowledged that he wanted to hear from his mother and sister. When questioned further, Gregory stipulated that his desire was to receive an audio tape from them rather than to converse in person or over the phone. Gregory was actually attempting to set up his own hierarchy of conditions in which he could gradually move closer to resuming a normal relationship with his mother. It was evident that he wanted to move slowly and to maintain as much control as possible. For his preferred condition, for example, he could shut off the tape at any time if and when his mother's words aroused anxiety within him. In desensitizing someone to overcome fear of another person, object, or situation, this is precisely the approach that is taken. The feared stimulus is gradually introduced in a form or setting that is initially most innocuous. Movement to a higher stimulus level of the feared object does not occur until the client is comfortable with and has mastered the previous level. In effect, this marked the very beginning of the planned process of desensitizing Gregory to innocuous aspects of his family and homeland. In this way, it was hoped, Gregory would gradually learn to discriminate between situations and people who presented a real danger to him (e.g., his father, who had not been treated) and those who presented no realistic threat. Irrational fears would consequently diminish and disappear in time as a function of such learning, referred to technically as counter-conditioning through reciprocal inhibition.

Later that afternoon, I received my own jolt of reality, which emphasized how little control over the total treatment package I really had. I called Bob McMahon to enthusiastically inform him of the substantial progress that Gregory was already making and of his desire to slowly rebuild his ties with his mother.

Bob interrupted. "Lenny, a visit has been set up with Gregory's mother for tomorrow at the U.S. mission to the United Nations."

"He's not ready for that yet," I insisted.

"We don't have a choice," countered Bob. "The State Department doesn't want to antagonize Zimbabwe. Zimbabwe is insisting on another visit now."

"This could set Gregory back, especially if it's going to be anything like the Christmas Eve visit."

"Unfortunately, they want everybody there. People from the State Department, the Zimbabwean mission, Legal Aid—and Dr. Heacock will be there. Yara will be bringing Gregory. I think you should go along too."

"I don't like it!" was my closing statement.

19. The Maternal Bond is Tested

Yara Fernandez, an attractive, statuesque woman of thirty-two, waited with Gregory and me for the State Department car to arrive. Yara, a social work supervisor at St. Christopher-Ottilie for three years, had picked up Gregory at the Kipling home earlier that morning. Their trip to my Jamaica office on that morning of January 14 had been uneventful. Gregory had seemed game about visiting with his mother, despite his stated preference for approaching this more gradually. If his mother had been brought to Jamaica for the visit, as is customary with supervised visits, it might have been a positive experience for all. There had been no contact between Mrs. Tanaka and Gregory in three weeks, and each seemed eager to reach out to the other. With his father half a world away, Gregory would now be able to relate on a one-to-one basis with his mother without impediment from a third party.

About 10:00 A.M. there was a call from the security guard in the lobby saying that a visitor from the State Department had just arrived. Gregory's mood and posture suddenly became rigid. He quietly but emphatically announced, "I don't want to go. I'll go another time."

When the woman from the State Department came in and heard of this latest turn of events, she became flustered and impatient. After more than a week of working with the Zimbabwean mission in arranging the visit, the people at State would have been totally frustrated if it fell through at the last moment. I was very tempted to say, "I told you so," but refrained. I, too, was looking forward to beginning the reconciliation process and to having the opportunity of meeting and talking with Mrs. Tanaka.

By now, however, Gregory had other ideas. He simply did not want to re-experience the very difficult visit of December 24. With all of those strangers watching, he had dared to confront his mother with his questions and his rage. Mrs. Tanaka had been forced into publicly repudiating Gregory's allegations about the beatings. This had made the ordeal much more unbearable for Gregory, as he was then viewed as the guilty party rather than as the victim. The Christmas Eve visit, rather than being an experience of conciliation and healing, had resensitized Gregory to feeling alone, misunderstood, and vulnerable. He did not want to be re-exposed to precisely the same circumstances as before.

Once Gregory had reneged, his resolve to cancel the visit grew stronger. Yara and I each appealed to him from a rational standpoint. "You'll just be saying hello, and you can leave whenever you're ready."

Gregory's thinking, however, was rapidly switching to the irrational mode, something that occurred whenever he was sufficiently frightened. His initial opposition to having another confrontation with his mother evolved into a pronounced fear that he would be abducted during the visit. Reasoning with him was not going to work.

Finally, I took Gregory aside and told him, "Even if you don't go to see your mother we have to leave the office. Let's go downstairs, and if you want to go back to Gary's house from there, you can."

With that, Gregory willingly put on his coat and went with me to the elevator, as Yara and the State Department woman trailed behind. When we went outside, the black government car and driver were waiting across the street. Gregory was the picture of ambivalence as he took one step in the direction of the car and then stepped away. He wanted to go, but he didn't want to go. He slowly approached the car as Yara entered and sat down in back. Gregory stood at the rear door of the car for about five minutes, equivocating on whether or not to get in.

We were getting nowhere. With great reluctance, I joined with Yara in forcing the issue. We physically nudged him into the car, and Gregory immediately fought back. He struggled as he sat between Yara and me in the back seat. The driver immediately started the car and took off.

The drive from Jamaica to the United Nations on First Avenue in Manhattan took approximately forty minutes. It was the longest, most excruciating car ride of my life. To begin with, I felt guilty about having had to mislead Gregory in order to get him to come to the car. Neither did I feel good about having resorted, however slightly, to physical force in situating him in the back seat. Gregory protested throughout the entire trip. His protest was physical rather than verbal, as he constantly attempted to extricate himself from the back seat. He attempted to go for one door, then attempted the other door, over and over again. Yara and I exerted considerable energy trying to keep him safely on the seat. I tried to explain to Gregory that the visit had been arranged based on his stated wish to resume contact with his mother, but that we did not have control over where and how the contact would be made. I was trying to convince him that we were really only carrying out his desires and, consequently, we weren't able just to call off everything in the middle. It appeared as if Gregory hadn't heard a word of what I was saying, as he relentlessly went for the doors. The strength of his tiny body was immense, as was his resolve.

At one point, I attempted to gain his attention by offering a wager. I said that I would bet him two dollars that he would be able to end the visit and leave as soon as he requested. Gregory seemed to be totally oblivious, and continued to struggle without interruption.

For the first twenty-five minutes of the ride, Gregory's struggle was a silent one. He showed no emotion, just a persistent determination to get out of the car. He was by no means totally out of control. He proceeded in a purposeful manner, and refrained from engaging in more extreme and dangerous measures that were available to him. He could have kicked at the windows, for example, but he didn't. He could have bitten my hand or Yara's to remove himself from our grasp, but he didn't.

When the car reached Franklin Delano Roosevelt Drive for the last leg of the trip, Gregory's demeanor changed abruptly, as though he recognized that he had entered "the last mile." His legs and arms thrashed much more wildly, and he began to scream and cry. He was genuinely and terribly frightened. He continued this higher-intensity struggle for the remainder of the trip. At one point, Yara and I looked at each other, exhausted from our endless ordeal, and simultaneously let go of Gregory. This effectively changed the location of Gregory's struggle to the front seat, where the State Department official and driver were seated, giving us a much-needed and well-deserved break.

As we turned the corner of East 42nd Street and First Avenue, the driver radioed to announce our imminent arrival at the U.S. mission to the U.N., which is located directly across the street from U.N. headquarters. When we approached a side entrance, doors opened automatically, and we drove into the driveway toward the garage beneath the building. The voyage was over. Columbus must have had an easier time!

We got out of the car—all of us, that is, but Gregory. He transformed from the persona of a caged tiger to that of a possum. No amount of coaxing could get him to come out of the car voluntarily. As it turned out, Mrs. Tanaka hadn't arrived yet, anyway, which provided a little more time to try to work things out. State Department official Bob Moeller came down to the garage with Dr. Heacock. After a brief, futile attempt at convincing Gregory to come out of the car, the two gentlemen looked at me with an unspoken request for me to attempt to move him physically. I immediately declared that I was through with my workout for the day and that any further attempts at getting Gregory beyond that point were going to be up to them.

"I hope you've been spending some time in the gym lately," I joked.

A call came down that Mrs. Tanaka and another woman from the Zimbabwean mission had just arrived. By this time everyone in the garage agreed that it was pointless to attempt to force Gregory to go upstairs. He could have his visit with his mother in the privacy of the car, with everyone else at a discreetly safe distance.

Moeller spoke by phone to Mrs. Tanaka, explaining the circumstances and the reason for having the visit in the basement garage. She was outraged.

Without hesitating a second, Mrs. Tanaka bolted from the room and ran for the door with her friend. Before anyone could dissuade her from leaving, she was racing up East 44th Street toward Second Avenue. Bob Moeller, a man in his mid-fifties, sprinted after her and finally caught up with her, but to no avail. Mrs. Tanaka was adamant about leaving. She would not allow her young son to humiliate her by assuming complete control and dictating the conditions of the visit.

All of us were given a brief glimpse of the kind of struggle for power that probably went on within the Tanaka family. Mrs. Tanaka—who hadn't seen her son in three weeks and who perhaps wouldn't have the chance to see him again for months, if not years—opted to cancel the visit rather than give in to Gregory. Could this be comparable to Gregory's refusal to give in to his father's demands, despite the threat of harsher and harsher physical punishment?

A consequence of the day's events was an immediate reappraisal of each other by State Department and St. Christopher-Ottilie staffs. In our struggle with Gregory, during which we demonstrated considerable care and restraint in handling him in a most professional manner, Yara and I had earned the respect and gratitude of the State Department people. They had been witnesses to the near-panic state to which Gregory had driven himself, and perhaps that raised the credibility of what we had been saying all along. We, on the other hand, had had a chance to see the sincere efforts on the part of people like Bob Moeller to handle Gregory with sensitivity and to extend themselves beyond the call of duty in an effort to bring forth a resolution of the case.

With his mother's departure from the building confirmed, Gregory acceded to going upstairs. He was treated royally by the staff and officials, and soon acted as if nothing had happened that morning. Sol Kutner, a veteran member of the U.S. mission, was gracious enough to take Dr. Heacock, Yara, and me to lunch in the cafeteria for dignitaries and officials at the United Nations. On our way to the cafeteria, Kutner gave us an impromptu tour, pointing out works of art, sculpture, and tapestries from all corners of the world. There was much enthusiasm and pride in his voice. Dining among those dignitaries from all over the world was truly a big thrill for me, but it didn't quite neutralize the unpleasant experiences of the morning.

That night, Mrs. Tanaka left for Zimbabwe, accompanied by her two daughters. Without knowing it, Gregory was truly alone now, perhaps never to see any of his family again. Our plans for gradually desensitizing Gregory to his mother and thereby beginning the process of reconciliation had to be scrapped. Our efforts now had to shift to urging Zimbabwe to designate and send a caretaker with whom we could work to establish him or her as a transitional object for Gregory. In order to accomplish this, we first had to convince the State Department of the correctness of such a move. State, in turn, would have the far more difficult task of convincing the Zimbabwean government to work cooperatively with us in this regard.

At the time, we had no way of knowing how remote the chances were of gaining Zimbabwe's cooperative participation in our plan. In a secret interview with a Zimbabwean government official taped on or about January 13, the hard-line, anti-American sentiment was most evident. The official referred to Gregory's initial placement by SSC as "abduction" and referred to SSC as "a child-abducting services group." He discounted the allegations of abuse, stating that this was a "small case blown out of proportion." He reiterated that there were institutions in Zimbabwe for taking care of such "misdemeanors," if in fact any wrongdoing had occurred. In closing, his stance toughened. "We continue to demand the immediate and unconditional release of Gregory to our mission in New York. The Zimbabwean government reserves the right to retaliate or reciprocate these acts of affront against its serenity and dignity. . . . Gregory should be released to his family, to Zimbabwe."

This did not bode well for a joint cooperative venture in the near future.

20. Abuse Revisited:
Searching for Trust

THE FOURTH therapy session was scheduled for Friday, January 15, the day after the abortive trip to the United Nations. I was quite apprehensive about how Gregory would act, considering the emotional events and disappointments of Thursday. I was particularly concerned about the fate of my relationship with Gregory. Would his trust in me evaporate if he thought I had betrayed him or deceived him in getting him to come to the U.N.? After our sustained physical struggle in the car, I was almost certain that I would be among the ranks of people not to be trusted.

I was astonished when Gregory entered my office without a trace of residual ill feeling about the preceding day. His only reference to Thursday's events was a remark that he had not felt ready to see his mother in person, but that he was open to speaking with her on the telephone. No mention was made of the struggle that we had in the State Department car. Had this child, who prided himself on remembering everything, forgotten or repressed yesterday's events? Or had he simply forgiven us and purposefully placed it out of his mind?

For the first time, Gregory agreed to be videotaped during our session. This was considered a significant indicator of movement toward an enhanced body image, which is correlated with a more positive self image. During his first few weeks in foster care, Gregory had been extremely camera shy, wanting no pictures to be taken of himself. He felt ashamed of himself and of his scarred body. Now, apparently, the shame was beginning to lift, but the feeling of vulnerability remained. During the taping, Gregory made believe he was a movie cartoon character named Howard the Duck being interviewed. In the movie, Howard is besieged and stalked by townspeople who attempt to broil him alive. Gregory's identification with Howard the Duck underscored the observation that he was still very frightened over being victimized by a malevolent mob that was totally biased against him, and was similar to his chronic fear of being betrayed by any and all Zimbabweans, who would turn him over to his father to be killed.

Nevertheless, Gregory was having a good time during the session, so I decided to extend it. This gave me the opportunity to begin administering some psychological tests that I had not been able to get around to when we were working on day-to-day crises. I administered a partial intelligence test, with a finding that Gregory possessed superior ability to abstract and generalize about environmental stimuli. Throughout the testing and the entire session, which lasted three full hours, Gregory was highly cooperative and receptive to the sustained attention he was receiving. He made no effort to terminate the session. On the contrary, I was forced to end it in order to have time for lunch and afternoon appointments. I told him it was time for him to go, and while we were waiting for Yara to pick him up, he dropped a bombshell.

"You lied to me," he asserted forcefully.

I was taken aback. I had absolutely no idea what he was referring to.

He repeated, "You lied to me. You owe me two dollars."

It took me a while to realize that Gregory was alluding to the two-dollar bet I had proposed in the car on the way to the U.N. on Thursday. He had never acknowledged hearing that comment of mine as he had been thoroughly absorbed in struggling to leave the car. Obviously, he had been taking in everything.

It was of interest that Gregory had made no reference to the bet throughout the three-hour session that had just ended, but he brought it up only after I terminated the session. Gregory had chosen to defer any grievances that he may have had against me until a most sensitive concern of his was raised by my termination of the session: feelings of abandonment. Up to this point, assumptions had been made about Gregory's tremendous fear for his safety and his rage over the treatment he had received in the past. Little attention had been given to an equally common nightmare of the abused child: fear of abandonment. Although an abused child is eager to secure a position of safety from further abuse, anxieties typically arise over the eventuality that once abusiveness stops, he will simply be forgotten or abandoned by the family. An abused child often interprets the cessation of abuse as a sure sign that the love and interest of his parents will subsequently vanish. He is, consequently, more intolerant of separation than are most children. He is highly insecure about significant figures or objects in his life remaining available to him. In technical terms, he has a poorly developed sense of object constancy. Conceivably, Gregory's experience of having his mother abort the visit on Thursday served to sensitize him to feeling abandoned. Those same feelings were now rekindled, except in this case it was the therapist who was perceived as abandoning him. It is no coincidence that later that day Gregory asked Gary if he and Joannie would adopt him.

Feelings of abandonment are the antithesis of feelings of trust. When we trust someone, we are convinced that that person would do nothing to hurt us. Rather, the trusted person is believed to be ever available when we need him, ever honest and ever reliable. Trust was what Gregory's post-session antics were all about. He demanded that I give him two dollars, or he would refuse to leave the office.

I quickly decided that I would not give in to or reinforce such blackmail. I refused to give him any money on the basis that the bet had never been made. Gregory had never agreed to the bet, and even if he had agreed, the cancellation of the visit left no opportunity for either of us to win or lose.

What had started out as a disagreement over whether or not a bet had been made quickly escalated, for Gregory, into another power struggle with authority. It was becoming evident that his struggle with autonomy and sense of self were the paramount issues in his life, and probably played significant roles in contributing to the physical abuse he received.

Now Gregory was prepared to have a major confrontation. He would assert his autonomy by refusing to leave with Yara. He surely was doing a good job of trying everyone's patience and generating negative feelings toward himself. Eventually Gregory succeeded in requiring the authority figure to resort to physical intervention as the confrontation escalated further. I assisted Yara in escorting Gregory into the elevator and down to the lobby of the building. We took hold of both his arms, but Gregory simply resisted more. He would not allow us to remove him from the lobby.

In a matter of seconds, Gregory was on the floor of the lobby, surrounded by curious and concerned spectators. As he lay on the floor, his eyes rolling and gyrating behind fluttering eyelids, Gregory appeared to enter a self-induced trance-like state. He was totally unreachable and uncommunicative. He had turned this power struggle with authority into a brief psychotic episode in which he temporarily shut off the world in a dissociative reaction. According to the American Psychiatric Association's *Diagnostic and Statistical Manual of Mental Disorders* (rev.), in a dissociative reaction, the individual defends against distressful thoughts or feelings through a "temporary alteration in the normally integrative function of consciousness. . . . The customary feeling of one's own reality is lost and replaced by a feeling of unreality."

Actually, Gregory was providing a first-hand demonstration of his adaptation of last resort to the brutal beatings he had received. It was reminiscent of his reaction on December 31, when he had climbed into the transfer file in Sea Cliff. Gregory's ultimate defense was to temporarily split off consciousness so that he would not have to feel physical pain or experience emotional anguish while his father beat him and other family members jeered. As such, this defense had probably served him very well and had helped him to survive an ordeal that others might not have survived. The problem now, however, was that this thin defense of last resort was being invoked at times when Gregory really didn't need it (i.e., when he did not face the kind of imminent danger he faced while tied up in the basement of his Jamaica Estates home). His response in the lobby was very disproportionate to the actual threat present; it had probably been set in motion when Gregory misperceived the import of his disagreement with me regarding the bet. Such disagreement quickly evolved into a potentially devastating threat to his self integrity and autonomy, perceived by Gregory to be comparable to the same threat when he was subjected to abuse.

Such a phenomenon is commonly seen in individuals suffering from a psychiatric disturbance known as Post-Traumatic Stress Disorder (PTSD). This disorder is often seen in combat veterans whose symptoms involve re-experiencing some psychologically traumatic event. The *Diagnostic and Statistical Manual of Mental Disorders* refers to the occurrence of

> dissociative-like states, lasting from a few minutes to several hours or even days, during which components of the event are relived and the individual behaves as though experiencing the event at that moment.[1]

This seems to be what was occurring in the lobby of the Jamaica office building. Arthur Green, M.D., referred to this phenomenon as it relates to the abused child as "retraumatization." He stated that in a hyper-vigilant state, the abused child

> is extremely sensitive to external events which might resemble the trauma in any way. These traumatic signals can trigger the circumvention of old feelings of helplessness and panic by initiating defensive activity. . . . Unfortunately, these emergency responses become over-generalized, and may occur in situations in which there is no objective danger.[2]

Dr. Green reported that as much as one half of a sample of abused children satisfied the criteria for PTSD. It certainly looked as though Gregory were suffering from it. Dr. Heacock had suspected as much, even before the incident in the lobby that all but confirmed it.

---

1. American Psychiatric Association, *Diagnostic and Statistical Manual of Mental Disorders*, (3rd ed. rev.). Washington, D.C.: American Psychiatric Association, 1987; p. 248.
2. Arthur H. Green, M.D., *Post-Traumatic Stress Disorders in Children* (S. Eth and R. Pynoos, eds.). Washington, D.C.: American Psychiatric Association, 1985; p. 145.

The issue of trust remained unresolved following the incident of January 15. The therapeutic relationship was at a critical crossroads. Gregory was prepared to risk total dissolution of the relationship if he could not find a sufficient basis for total trust. Would I honor what he thought I said regarding the bet? Would I still show unconditional acceptance of him despite his oppositional behavior? How much did I really want the relationship to continue? Would I abandon him? These were the questions that had to be answered for Gregory.

For the next two days, Gregory refused to see me or talk with me. Finally, I asked Gary to inform him that I would be coming to visit with Gary's family on January 18 and would be interested in speaking with Gregory if he agreed. When I arrived, Gregory remained upstairs watching television, refusing to come down to greet me. It had all the trappings of the standoff in the U.S. mission garage between Gregory and his mother. He had tested her on that day, and most probably drawn the inference that she didn't care enough about him to see him on his terms. Any feeling of abandonment was thereby confirmed. Now Gregory was testing whether I, too, was inclined to abandon him. I was not, and I showed it by going upstairs and sitting in the room with him, even though he still refused to talk with me. The important message I was attempting to give was that I would remain available to him regardless of any disagreements or arguments that we might have. I would not fall into the trap of slipping into yet another power struggle with him. Nothing was said between us for at least twenty or thirty minutes as we silently watched a movie on television. Then Gregory sneezed.

"God bless you," I said automatically.

"Thank you," Gregory replied—reflecting an upbringing that stressed good manners.

That simple exchange broke the ice. It entailed neither of us waving a white flag of surrender. Gregory seemed greatly relieved. He accepted my request for him to teach me a computer game, which quickly established him in the esteemed role of teacher. Thus there was no need for him to continue to battle for autonomy, and Gregory was able to lower his defenses. This made it much easier for me eventually to broach the subject of our infamous bet. Rather than re-hash our positions, I felt this was a great opportunity to introduce the principle of compromise.

"You think I owe you two dollars," I said. "I think I owe you nothing. We have a disagreement, but I don't want that disagreement to hurt our friendship. Nothing is worth hurting our friendship. The best thing to do in a case like this is to compromise."

"What is a compromise?" Gregory asked.

"It's when each person gives a little to the other person. Each tries to come a little closer to what the other person wants. What would be a good compromise for us?" I asked.

Gregory could not come up with an answer. The notion of compromise was foreign to him, but he was very interested in understanding more about it.

"How about my giving you one dollar instead of two?" I asked. "That's halfway between what each of us thinks I owe you."

Gregory thought it over and, with a smile, accepted my dollar. Our crisis was over, but not because of one of us exerting our power over the other. An important lesson had been learned. Differences with authority figures need not elicit the stoic, extremely oppositional, regressive responses that had been such important parts of Gregory's behavioral repertoire in the past. Thereafter, compromise became a much-used approach when there were differences of opinion in Gary's home. Gary later informed me that Gregory often spontaneously came up with compromise solutions when he was at odds with either Gary or Joannie. Of course, eventually he would have to learn that compromise isn't always possible, but even the attempt at compromise promised to have a conciliatory effect on all parties involved.

Gregory's struggle in search of someone to trust was not uncommon for an abused child. The abused child's primary experience with a potential love object, his parents, is tainted by the experience of repeatedly being hurt and maligned. In an attempt to maintain the fantasy of having a good parent, he resorts to primitive psychological defenses. He denies the parents' badness, projects such badness onto himself or others, and attempts to preserve an idealized image of a good parent. The abused child approaches the therapist as if he were a substitute for his parent. He is consequently distrustful and suspicious at first, but this is soon replaced by an idealized view. At this stage, the child fantasizes that the therapist will be everything that his parent wasn't (i.e., accepting and loving). Of course, this sets the stage for a big disappointment when the child discovers that the therapist is not living up to expectations. The ensuing angry reaction by the child is the kind of response given by Gregory when he felt let down by me. With past experience as his guide, the abused child expects retaliatory action from the therapist or substitute parent as he projects his own anger onto the therapist. Here, one hopes, is where therapy departs from the child's past history of disturbed object relations. The therapist does not retaliate as expected, thus negating the need for the child to engage in aggressive and/or oppositional counter-phobic behavior. The cycle that perpetuates provocative behavior leading to abusive parental reaction is thereby disrupted. When Gregory saw that I was more interested in compromise than in retaliation, he was given a significant, concrete basis on which to build trust.

During the first three weeks of treatment, Gregory concocted another test to determine whether or not I was worthy of his trust. During an early session, I attempted to convince him to spend some time with a female colleague, for the purpose of additional psychological testing. In an effort to coax him, I noted that she was very pretty as well as very friendly. Big mistake!

Immediately, Gregory jumped to the conclusion that I was having an affair with this woman. From that point on, he repeatedly raised that allegation, threatening to tell my wife, and, in fact, asking to speak with her on the phone. What contributed to Gregory's misperception was a telephone conversation he had overhead between Bob McMahon's secretary and me. His secretary, Mary Paulis, a wonderful, dedicated woman, is known affectionately by the name "Honey." When Gregory heard me talking to a Honey who, by my own admission, wasn't my wife, his suspicions of my infidelity were confirmed. It didn't help matters that, prior to placement, his parents had taken him to see the movie *Fatal Attraction*. It may be surmised that he thought, "How can I trust anybody who lies and is unfaithful to his own wife?"

This running theme provided many opportunities in subsequent sessions for exploring and defining such important aspects of enduring relationships as love, sincerity, honesty, and loyalty. Gregory would have to master the criteria for determining whom to trust later on if he was ever going to take the risk of returning to Zimbabwe.

21. Progress is Noted

PRIOR TO session number six on January 20, Gary Kipling called with some disconcerting news. Gregory's behavior at home was deteriorating. In a number of ways, Gregory was exhibiting a pattern very similar to what he had probably shown with his natural family. To begin with, he had been bullying Gary's four-year-old son, Adam, taking away his games and otherwise taunting him. Gregory had become extremely critical of Adam, readily blaming him and suggesting that he should be harshly punished. Earlier in the month, Gregory had alleged that Adam had robbed his piggy bank and should be electrocuted. This attitude and treatment of Adam paralleled the hostility that he had exhibited toward his sister Kim prior to Kim's returning to her mother. It demonstrated the very deep resentment he felt and his desire to have others treated as harshly as he had been treated. For Gregory, authority had always seemed to treat him unfairly.

Oppositional stances against authority appeared in various situations, but were mild in comparison to what Gregory was capable of doing. When he disliked what Joannie Kipling was telling him to do, he held his ears. He still resorted to his possum routine as a means of demonstrating displeasure (e.g., he refused to leave the car when on a shopping trip). His antagonistic feelings toward educational endeavors was manifested by his recalcitrance when with his tutor. On one occasion, Gregory had hidden under the bed in an attempt to avoid having a lesson.

More alarming than Gregory's behavioral reversals was the implication that Dr. Heacock might be considering prescribing a small dosage of a strong tranquilizer with anti-psychotic action. There had been prior concern voiced by Dr. Heacock that Gregory's reference to a little Martian friend was close to being delusional. It was difficult, however, to estimate to what extent such references were attributable to hallucinatory experiences rather than to Gregory's rich fantasy life and a desire to "put people on." Delusional-type verbalizations, initially viewed as benign, assumed a more pathological aspect, however, in the context of anti-social, impulsive, and/or regressive behavior. I was personally against the idea of giving Gregory psychotropic medication, based on my observations of him during therapy sessions. Fortunately, the matter never came to a conflict between us mental health professionals, as Gregory soon began to show some favorable clinical signs of improvement.

Of significance was the observation that Gregory seemed more sociable. He seemed to seek out and derive more from social inter-actions with the Kipling children and with many adults. Despite still slipping into confrontations with authority, he was quick to apologize, underscoring his great desire to maintain a positive relationship with Gary and Joannie.

Just as significant was Gregory's newly found readiness to verbalize his dissatisfactions rather than to act them out. Better impulse control and higher tolerance of frustration were also noted. Gregory apparently was learning to express anger and aggression in a socialized manner. This was attributable in part to his exposure to attitudes and behavioral models in his foster home and in therapy, which emphasized self-control through a reflective, rational approach in dealing with frustrations and with problems. Gregory now identified with a much less aggressive model than before; hence the level of his own aggression and impulsivity declined.

Self-esteem, an oft-mentioned goal of psychotherapy, is difficult to measure. Everything from self-report inventories to self-statements to changes in behavior or affect is used to indicate progress or lack of progress in this crucial area. By the end of January and during the first few days of February, it was quite evident that Gregory was much more accepting of himself than he had been a month earlier. He was even beginning to like himself. He now proudly allowed himself to be videotaped or photographed. Whereas he had formerly refused to allow anyone to see him undressed, he now requested to take a shower with Gary so that he could feel like one of the guys. During the tenth session, on February 3, Gregory stated that he no longer had any marks left from his beatings, and was therefore not sensitive about having his shirt off. He felt so confident and good about himself that he actually asked when he might discontinue his in-home tutoring and begin attending regular school. This was from a child whose entire school career had been one of repeated failure.

The enhancement of self-esteem is a direct outgrowth of the positive regard shown an abused child, something that is usually a novel experience for him. The child slowly begins to view himself the way his new friends appreciate him. This does not happen overnight. The change gradually takes hold after days, weeks, or sometimes months of exposure to consistent, convincing adults expressing their genuine acceptance of and admiration for the child.

Another source of heightened self-esteem pertains to an increased sense of self-efficacy—the belief that one can cope with almost any eventuality that comes his way. Such a belief is built on prior experience in successfully mastering problematic situations. When Gregory came into foster care, his feeling of self-efficacy was nil. He had been someone who could do no right. Remember, at our first session he announced that the only thing he could do well was "remember." Now, in early February, he prided himself on a model car he had completed and in math problems he had solved. A most important contributor to his sense of self-efficacy was the opportunity he was being given to exercise a greater say in his own fate. He was enjoying far more freedom to choose among matters of concern to him, and he did not have to resort to futile, tragic power struggles in order to gain such personal control. For a child who feels powerless, overwhelmed, and defeated, the greatest "medicine" that can be given is the introduction of choice in his life.

By early February, progress toward each of the treatment goals was noted. Dr. Heacock agreed that clinical gains had occurred. Yet there was still no change in Gregory's position on returning to Zimbabwe. He still did not want to leave, but there were some tiny cracks in his previously rigid stance. He was more willing now to talk about Zimbabwe and about living there. During a videotaping session on February 1, Gregory at first reiterated his opposition to living in Zimbabwe, but subsequently he allowed me to pose a hypothetical question.

"If you had to live in Zimbabwe, would you prefer living with your family or with another family?" I asked.

Gregory replied that his preference would be to live with another family. Previously, he would not have entertained any notion of answering such a question.

Gregory later emphasized that it was not fear that was keeping him from returning to Zimbabwe. "I just don't want to live there, that's all," was the only reason he gave. Gone was the total state of terror of a month ago.

Informally, Gregory became more willing to let such phrases as "When you return to Zimbabwe . . ." go unchallenged. During the latter part of January, I took Gregory out to Wendy's for lunch. His explorations in the glove compartment of my car led to his discovery of my sunglasses. He asked and was given permission to put them on. He was so impressed by the way he looked in them that he asked if he could wear them in the restaurant. Over hamburgers, fries, and cokes, I promised Gregory that I would let him have the glasses when "the time came for us to say goodbye for a long time."

Gregory hesitated for a moment, then, with a big smile, inquired, "You mean, when I go to Zimbabwe?"

Such a thought no longer terrified Gregory, but he was still adamantly opposed to any move. Short-term individual psychotherapy alone would not be sufficient to promote a change in Gregory's attitude regarding going to Zimbabwe. The help of others, Zimbabweans in particular, would be required, as I had indicated back on January 5, when I was interviewed at NBC.

22. A Special Foster Home

WITH GREGORY showing gains in self-esteem, impulse control, and frustration tolerance, and with his ability to relate positively to authority, he looked and acted more and more like any nine-year-old child. He blended in beautifully during the one month that he lived with Gary and Joannie Kipling and their sons. Gregory's emotional condition had stabilized considerably, but his future was still very clouded. Still opposed to returning to Zimbabwe, Gregory fantasized about another alternative: being adopted and remaining with the Kiplings for the remainder of his childhood. The day after his mother left for Zimbabwe, Gregory asked Gary if he could be adopted.

After living through an extremely unsettled, unpredictable January, Gregory showed signs of wanting to settle down to lead a normal existence. He asked to be enrolled in school and to join regular recreation programs. Although confiding that he loved his mother, he still saw no viable path to resuming a safe life with her. His stay in foster care was beginning to look like it would go on indefinitely. It was decided that a move back to his initial foster home in Freeport would be best for a number of reasons.

We did not want to inadvertently support Gary's growing fantasy of permanently remaining with the Kiplings. The idea was unrealistic, and would only divert Gregory from the very difficult task of reconciling his mixed feelings about his natural family. Staying with the Kiplings would probably prolong that task.

Furthermore, the Kiplings were not prepared for a long-term foster care arrangement. During the month of January, their work and personal schedules had been sacrificed to meet the rapidly changing demands that Gregory's case required. Gary had been forced to sharply curtail his work as assistant executive director for St. Christopher-Ottilie. Joannie's schedule had been affected significantly, and she had prior plans to leave New York to be with relatives for several weeks.

If Gregory was to stay in the U.S. for a prolonged period of time, he required a foster care setting prepared to provide him with normalized conditions and routines. As per standard St. Christopher-Ottilie policy, every effort should be made to situate a child in a household with religious and racial backgrounds comparable to those of the child. In this case, a move back to the first foster home would enable Gregory to be with a black family again. (It should be emphasized, however, that Gregory never appeared to view the racial difference between the Kiplings and him as an issue. He never was heard to utter one comment that was even remotely connected with race.)

With little fanfare and only minimal reluctance on Gregory's part, he moved back to his initial foster home on February 1. On the day of the move, he told of his plans to write a book entitled *My Life with Jeremy*. The brief friendship that Gregory had enjoyed with the Kipling's older boy, Jeremy, was but one of the many significant blessings that Gregory had experienced in his time with the Kiplings.

Gary and Joannie Kipling had been thrust into the role of foster parents with no prior notice on New Year's Eve. Gary, a member of the St. Christopher-Ottilie staff for over ten years, epitomized the qualities that helped propel the agency into a leadership position. Intelligent and knowledgeable, a fine administrator, Gary is, above all else, deeply compassionate and sensitive to the needs of young children. He is a loyal team player, and did not hesitate to offer his home and his family to help out in a time of crisis. Gary and Joannie had had ample parenting experience with their own children, Jeremy and Adam, but they had had no prior experience as foster parents. So what's the difference?

In many respects, there are and should be no differences between one's approach to parenting and foster parenting. In either case, a child needs love, understanding, unconditional acceptance, a feeling of belonging, security, protection, nurturance, and guidance. A child needs to feel that he is living in a friendly, benevolent, orderly, and predictable environment so that he may expend his full energies in the direction of personal growth and self-actualization. In the case of most children sent into foster care, their attention is diverted to questions of survival and self-protection. They have been previously denied the luxury of living in an environment where all of their physical and emotional needs are reliably met. In attempting to adapt to dysfunctional family environments, many of these children develop dysfunctional behaviors and become emotionally disturbed. When a child first moves into a foster home, he may feel initial relief in escaping from an abusive natural-family environment, but he soon opposes the foster parents' efforts to function as substitute parents. He begins to project his natural parents' negative qualities onto the foster parents and acts out unresolved family conflicts in the foster home.

One of the toughest aspects of being a foster parent is having to open your heart and home to a child, knowing it will be for only a brief time. People get attached to each other. In showing love and caring, the foster parent and child can't help but become emotionally attached. The closer the attachment, the more difficult the separation. All parties, by necessity, are thereby thrust into an emotional roller coaster that can be quite difficult to handle.

Foster parents are instructed to treat a foster child as though he were one of the family, but this is easier said than done. Natural children of the foster parents often quietly or overtly resent the intrusion of the foster child. The foster child often introduces unsettling conflict into the household, thus destroying its prior tranquility. Yet all are asked to accept the child and to love the child unconditionally. This is too much to ask of some foster parents, who eventually become overwhelmed by the pressures that the foster child has added and ask for his removal. All too often, the cycle of rejection and abandonment begun with the natural family is recapitulated in the child's foster care experience.

Gary and Joannie had been up to the challenge posed by Gregory's placement in their home. Their love of children extended naturally and automatically to him. Gregory felt the love that the Kiplings extended to him. He felt their calmness and serenity, in sharp contrast to the near-panic state in which he had been prior to placement. The Kiplings gave Gregory a semblance of order and control in his life, but not on his terms of blackmail. They presented firm limits and imposed natural consequences to his positive and negative actions. Communication had replaced intimidation and repression. Gregory had learned that problems could in fact be resolved by talking them out. The lessons of compromise had been reinforced as well.

Above all, Gregory was given new role models with whom to identify. He had benefited tremendously from observing an adult male exert his authority not through resorting to a display of power, but by relying upon reason and common sense while upholding the dignity of all family members. He had benefited from sharing in the love of a family unfettered by scapegoating and intimidation. Finally, he had gained from the experience of having other children readily accept him as a friend and share so openly with him. The Kipling home had been a special foster home, indeed. In one short month, the Kiplings had demonstrated how crucial and therapeutic a role the foster family plays in the life of a frightened, lonely, and disillusioned child separated from his natural family.

23. Finding Solutions: Child's Play

B EFORE GREGORY could seriously consider returning to
Zimbabwe and salvaging his family ties, he had first to
make some sense out of the past so that he could ascertain whether
there was any hope for real change in his future. Despite his avowed
love of his mother and his ties to his sisters, it would be unthinkable
to go back to a situation in which he would again be scapegoated
and left unprotected. Deeply painful feelings associated with the
abusive past precluded Gregory from engaging in direct, meaningful
discussions analyzing what went wrong. On the contrary, Gregory
was quite reluctant to speak about his future with his family.
Another way of addressing vital questions about family was needed.
That alternative path was through thematic play, and Gregory gladly
and enthusiastically jumped on it when it was offered.

Children readily project their interests, concerns, and conflicts
into their fantasy play. In play the stakes are not high; danger is
non-existent. Imagination and creativity are available for the child
to use as he pleases in choosing any ending to his play drama; the
inhibiting component of reality can be temporarily ignored. In play,
the child is the boss. He structures all the action to suit his perception of the world and his wishes for a modified world. Through
Gregory's play we were able to gain a clearer understanding of both
the world he lived in before placement and the world he wished to
live in if and when he returned to Zimbabwe.

As stated in an earlier chapter, Gregory's initial thematic play provided an opportunity for him to gain a cathartic release of his pent-up rage and a coinciding outlet within which his revenge fantasies could find expression. Such play was both stimulating and satisfying to Gregory, but it offered no new answers to vexing questions.

Meaningful direction for the future first appeared in Gregory's play during the sixth therapy session, on January 20. Our play with a set of wooden blocks and some matchbox cars led to discoveries concerning knowing when to take risks and when to avoid dangerous situations. Gregory became engrossed in building an intricate network of ramps out of the blocks. He joyfully guided a matchbox car up and down the ramps until it reached the longest ramp, which led to the final destination. I likewise guided my matchbox car to the same point, but proceeded no further. I portrayed the driver of my car as being too frightened to cross the ominous-looking final ramp. The driver announced that he was afraid of falling off the ramp. Hearing this, Gregory brought his car and driver to the aid of my driver. Gregory's driver bravely guided my driver across the ramp. Afterward, I asked Gregory about his driver's bravery, and he divulged its source.

"He sent a remote-controlled car to test it [the ramp] out first."

The analogy to Gregory's conflict over returning home was obvious. Gregory was in search of advanced proof via some form of test probe that things would be safe for him when he crossed his "ramp" to Zimbabwe. At this early stage of the game, the source and form of such proof was unknown, but through play, Gregory was a bit more focused about what he was looking for. Eventually, he would need incontrovertible evidence guaranteeing his safety.

Play during two other sessions proved crucial to Gregory's efforts to gain clarification and a better understanding of his mother's failure to protect him from his father. The question of why his mother had failed to take a more active role in protecting him or in attempting to influence Mr. Tanaka to change his ways had to be addressed before Gregory could ever consider rejoining Mrs. Tanaka. In session eight, on January 27, Gregory engaged in thematic play involving anatomically explicit dolls. Gregory's interest and curiosity about heterosexual relationships seemed precocious for his age, and it surfaced in a number of our discussions. In his play, he depicted the woman as being easily exploited, sexually and otherwise, due to weakness and loneliness. The latter quality, in his view, served to make her vulnerable to eventually giving in to and identifying with the male aggressor. Specifically, a married woman was portrayed as initially resisting the approaches of a rapist, only to eventually yield to him and consent to having sex because she was lonely.

Such a portrayal of the adult female as weak and at the mercy of the male was extended in the eleventh therapy session, on February 8. Thematic play with family puppets came as close to mirroring Gregory's true life situation as possible. In the play, the father threatened to kill his son unless the latter complied with the demand to ride a horse. Once threatened, the child tried to jump out of the window, and was rescued by a fireman who caught him. The child's mother, rather than assist in the rescue, preferred to remain with her husband and joined him in his new residence, Hell. Some time later, however, the mother made a significant discovery: her husband was dead. She immediately returned to her son, and a reconciliation between mother and son ensued. Obviously, she had refrained from helping her son earlier only because of her considerable fear of and dependency on her husband. (Gregory explained that the mother needed to stay with her husband because she didn't have a job.)

A modified view of his mother was emerging from Gregory's play. She was regarded as a terrified victim in her own right, with little if any status or power. Gregory was now beginning to look at his mother in a more benevolent, sympathetic light. Perhaps his anger and exasperation with her for failing to protect him was diminishing.

Toward the end of the same session, Gregory's serendipitous discovery of a book on my desk led to significant revelations for him concerning his father's abusive behavior. The book, *Changing the Abusive Parent,* intrigued Gregory, and he inquired about it. This gave me an unplanned opportunity to talk about the phenomenon of child abuse for the first time. I explained that the book and other materials were used in a weekly parent training group that I conducted at St. Christopher-Ottilie. The group is open to any parent with a child in foster care, including many who have been implicated in abuse. Gregory was amazed by the discovery that many other children were similarly abused, and, more significantly, that many abusive and neglectful parents engage in rehabilitative efforts to change their child-rearing attitudes and practices. That such adults might change to the extent that they could resume their parental roles was an important revelation to Gregory, who was, nevertheless, still skeptical.

Two days later, however, in response to my question about whether he felt it was possible for his father to learn new, non-abusive ways of dealing with his children, Gregory said, "Maybe there's a teensy chance." He then astounded me by suggesting that I go to Zimbabwe (without him) to do parent training with both his parents. I countered by suggesting that there might be someone like me who lives in Zimbabwe who could train his parents. Gregory encouraged me to find out if there was such a person available. He was finally ready to look for help from a Zimbabwean.

Gregory's readiness to believe that change was possible grew markedly during the ensuing week. His puppet play during the thirteenth session, on February 17, demonstrated how far he had come in that regard. The protagonist in this play had a bad temper, which manifested itself in his hurting others. A metamorphosis occurred after consulting an elderly, wise priest who formerly had the same problem himself. It took a while for the others in the play to believe that the protagonist was free of his temper problem, but eventually he proved it to everyone. Gregory now seemed able to accept the possibility that, with appropriate training, durable change could occur. At the end of the session, Gregory brought up our discussion of the parent training group from the previous week.

"I thought you were making that up," he confessed. "Do you really send the kids back home?"

Gregory had obviously done much thinking about his situation, and about the prospects of his parents' changing sufficiently to allow him to someday rejoin the family. It was still a long shot, but for the first time in a long time there was a ray of hope.

I never got to explain much of the specifics of the content of the parent training program to Gregory. Certainly, positive methods of discipline and communication are topics that are stressed. I didn't mention that his father might require something more intensive than a parent training group, such as individual psychotherapy. It would be most helpful if his father could be taught about the dynamics behind his proclivity to abuse Gregory. Was Mr. Tanaka simply resorting to tried-and-true practices that had been used on him as a child and which were regarded as acceptable by his Zimbabwean neighbors? Or did psychological factors play a role in compelling him to act as he did? In targeting Gregory as the family scapegoat, was he beating a part of himself when he was whipping his child?

In most cases of scapegoating, the scapegoated child is the one who is most closely identified with the abusing parent. The child elicits negative feelings in the parent as he reminds the parent of traits in himself that he despises. The parent reacts defensively by projecting such unacceptable traits onto his child. It would remain for Mr. Tanaka and his therapist to determine whether similar dynamics applied to him. Certainly other psychological, historical, and environmental factors would be explored as well. Mr. Tanaka's motivation or lack of motivation to approach training or therapy openly and nondefensively would be a crucial variable contributing to the ultimate success or failure of this quest for change, in which Gregory now believed.

It is significant to note that during this period of tremendous clinical gain witnessed in the sessions of February 8, 10, and 17, Gregory exhibited a noticeable increase in oppositional behavior and dysphoric mood in his foster home. He refused to comply with parental requests, went on a brief "hunger strike," and was highly resistant to his tutor. He was described by his tutor as "acting crazy" on Mondays and Wednesdays prior to attending therapy sessions, but acting in a more subdued fashion on Tuesdays and Thursdays, the days following his therapy sessions.

Furthermore, his foster mother observed Gregory whimpering at bedtime. I felt that these difficulties at home reflected the growing inner conflict precipitated by Gregory's new insights in therapy. Before those insights, Gregory's position was uncomplicated: he was safe and comfortable in his foster home, and entertained no thought of leaving. Thus, he was not required to contemplate risk-taking and "what if" thinking. Now, however, he was in conflict, struggling to find direction in seeking the right path. The question of returning to Zimbabwe was now a live issue for Gregory, and this was its toll, both behaviorally and emotionally.

24. A Call from Mom,
A Visitor from Home

BY MID-FEBRUARY, Gregory was ready for the last phase of the treatment plan that had been mapped out in early January. He was now primed to engage in the process of desensitization. In this process, the child's irrational fears are removed through gradual exposure to the object of his fears. In Gregory's case, his rational fear of his father was generalized to an irrational fear of all Zimbabweans. In order for the latter fear to be removed, Gregory needed to have direct, positive, and innocuous experiences with at least one person from Zimbabwe who could later serve as a protective transitional object for Gregory when he left foster care and America.

Of equal importance was the need for Gregory to resume contact with his mother, who represented the strongest bond that Gregory had to anyone from his homeland. To be successful, such contacts would have to be far less confrontational than were the last visits, on December 24 and January 14. A renewed attempt at repairing family ties had to begin much more slowly and gradually. The main risk to avoid in a desensitization program is resensitizing or heightening irrational fears by exposing the child too quickly or too intensely to the feared object. That is precisely what occurred on December 24 and January 14, and had resulted in setbacks for Gregory.

Fortuitous timing was needed, and our wish was granted. All through January and early February, treatment had been handicapped by our inability to enlist the cooperative participation of the Zimbabwean government or Gregory's mother. State Department officials worked tirelessly in appealing for cooperation from Zimbabwe. Where once the St. Christopher-Ottilie people had tried to educate and win over the State Department, now it was the State Department that tried to educate and win over the Zimbabwean government. Its mission was to sway the Zimbabweans away from the political ramifications of the case and impress upon them the clinical and personal requirements for resolution of the case. In short, the Zimbabweans had to start trusting us and our motives. Our function was not to abduct children, as they had claimed. Politically, there was no intent to embarrass or demean Zimbabwe. We were not contesting their claim that they had a child welfare system equal to ours. The diplomatic task of the State Department was to get these messages across convincingly. This was no easy task.

We at St. Christopher-Ottilie had been requesting involvement with the Zimbabweans since the first week of January. We had beseeched the State Department to arrange direct contact, but any efforts they had made had been unsuccessful. At the State Department's urging, Bob McMahon telexed the Zimbabwean Ministry of Social Welfare on January 15 to initiate consultation with them, but no response had been received. At that point in time, the Zimbabwean government still disavowed the existence of any problem involving child abuse by Mr. Tanaka. At about the same time, the secret interview referred to previously was conducted by one of the local news stations. In it, a Zimbabwean government official expressed a hard-line, anti-American sentiment. For whatever reason, the station never aired the interview.

About a week later, on January 21, Zimbabwe finally sent a government official to meet with us and Gregory. His name was Jonathan, and when he arrived at my Jamaica office he was extremely quiet, tense, and reserved. He said very little to any of us, but had a pleasant private meeting with Gregory. It was evident that Jonathan had been sent to assess Gregory's status, but not to collaborate in any way with us. Following his meeting with Jonathan, Gregory informed me that the topic of his return to Zimbabwe had not been raised. They had talked about the possibility of visiting

Washington, D.C., which appealed to Gregory as long as Gary or I accompanied him. It was a moot question, however, since none of us ever heard from Jonathan again. Several days later, on January 25, a *New York Post* article, referring most probably to Jonathan, quoted an unnamed Zimbabwean official as stating that Gregory was being held against his wishes. Allusions were made to his "longing to see his friends" in Zimbabwe.

This distant, adversarial position was maintained by Zimbabwe through the middle of February. Then a dramatic change occurred.

Sol Kutner of the State Department called me on February 16 and informed me that Gregory's mother had requested a phone conversation with Gregory. Actually, the Zimbabwean government in Harare had made the request in her behalf to American embassy officials there, who in turn had passed on word to the State Department in Washington.

I voiced my concern that Gregory might be taken by surprise by the call, which was to occur later the same day. I asked if the call could wait until the next day, after I had had the opportunity to better prepare him for it. Such a decision was out of Kutner's hands, and he so informed me. In closing, I urged that someone attempt to coach Mrs. Tanaka in order to avoid another confrontation and a resensitization setback for Gregory.

"Mrs. Tanaka should give Gregory the message that she misses him, that she realizes there were family problems in the past, and that she is working to correct them," I pleaded.

I very much doubt that my message for Mrs. Tanaka was received by her. My plea for a delay of the phone contact was not honored. A call from Mrs. Tanaka was put through to Gregory at his foster home later that afternoon. The only people who were privy to the details of the conversation were Gregory and his mother.

When Gregory arrived for his therapy session the next day, he acknowledged having spoken with his mother for about forty-five minutes. The only things he consented to tell me about the conversation were that he had asked her if she would let his father hit him again and whether his father was living apart from the family now. Gregory was not clear on what answers, if any, his mother had given him. He inferred from her remarks that she was living with an uncle, but he was not sure about this.

Gregory had little more to say about the conversation, but emphatically indicated that he would like to try to call her the following Monday, February 22. He added that he would welcome my talking to her as well. From the limited data available, I concluded that this first direct contact with his mother in almost two months had been a positive experience for Gregory.

On Friday, February 19, Bob Moeller called to inform me of two other significant developments during this watershed week. He said that a male social worker from Zimbabwe would be arriving in New York within twenty-four hours and would meet with Gregory on Sunday. Second, two State Department psychiatrists would come from Washington on Monday to speak with Gregory, Dr. Heacock, and me to ascertain Gregory's status.

The Zimbabwean arrived on Saturday as scheduled, and was driven to the foster home to meet Gregory on Sunday. Isaac Mukaro, a handsome, diminutive, soft-spoken, self-assured black man, appeared to be in his early thirties. He was very low-key and sensitive in his demeanor; a more appropriate selection for the task at hand could not have been made. Here was a Zimbabwean male of professional stature who was the direct antithesis of the persona portrayed by Gregory's father.

Mukaro was both physically and behaviorally non-threatening as he entered the foster home and shook hands with Gregory. He wore a big smile that expressed warmth and understanding, and was careful to avoid moving too quickly. He asked Gregory if he wanted to see some pictures and other things that he had brought from home in Zimbabwe. Gregory looked with interest at pictures of his mother and sisters, but was most interested in a note sent by a chum named Jeffrey. Pleasant emotions associated with those happy earlier years in Zimbabwe were evoked.

After some additional exchanges of factual information about his sister, Gregory felt comfortable enough to bring up his major concern.

"What about my father? Where is he? Is he living with my mother?" Gregory asked in rapid succession.

Mukaro replied that Gregory's father was not presently with his mother.

"Are they putting my father in jail?" Gregory asked. "He should be in jail."

"Your father may have to go to jail. That will be decided," answered Mukaro.

Gregory seemed satisfied with Isaac Mukaro's last answer. Here was someone of importance from his homeland who was giving credibility to his allegations of abuse. "They're sending him to jail," he thought. "They must believe me!"

The two spent a very pleasant afternoon together. Gregory took readily to his new friend, who offered to have him as a house guest for a while when Gregory returned to Zimbabwe the following Sunday.

"Will you come with me?" Mukaro asked. "You can meet my family. I have a son about your age."

Gregory didn't reply.

Rather than press further, Mukaro wisely backed off and said, "Don't decide just now. Think about it, and you can let me know later in the week."

The visit ended on that note. It had been an astounding session. Gregory had found in Mukaro a countryman of position who could provide him protection. Even in this first meeting, Gregory determined that he could trust the Zimbabwean. His experiences of learning to trust during the past two months were now reaping dividends. No longer did he believe that any and all Zimbabweans would act as though they were agents of his father. He was now able to discriminate between the dangerous and the non-dangerous, the trustworthy and the non-trustworthy.

The next day, Monday, February 22, Gregory excitedly barged into my office for his scheduled therapy session and announced, "This Sunday is my last day here."

I was floored and speechless.

Gregory proceeded. "I want to go back to Zimbabwe this Sunday. I'll write. I'll live with the social worker from Zimbabwe for a little while. His name is Isaac. I met him yesterday. After a while, I will move to my mother's."

I attempted to gain some understanding of the reasons for Gregory's change of heart, but I was wary of sounding pessimistic or of putting a damper on these exciting plans in any way.

"What made you decide to go back?" I asked.

"I can't tell you."

"Come on, Gregory, I'm interested in knowing. You used to be so afraid of going back, and now you're not. What made the difference?"

"I'm still afraid, but I'm ready to go now," he said in mature, realistic fashion.

"So what changed things?" I persisted.

"I just can't tell you," Gregory repeated, now somewhat annoyed.

At that rebuff I suspended any further effort at understanding the basis for Gregory's decision. Gregory recalled that we had planned to call his mother this day and asked if I would call. What followed was my first attempt at reaching Africa by telephone.

For the next twenty minutes I spoke with a number of telephone operators, all of whom were unable to reach the number that Gregory had provided. It was a first for them, too. We were about to give up when, finally, I heard a ring on the other end. A woman's voice answered.

I asked for Mrs. Tanaka, who had to be called from outside. When she got on the phone I started to explain who I was. But Gregory grabbed the phone out of my hands to say hello.

"I decided to come home," he said.

Naturally, I could hear only Gregory's part of the ensuing conversation. This is how some of it sounded to me:

"Where is Daddy?"

(No apparent answer from mother.)

"Will I have to live with him? . . . I'm not living with him. I don't want to live with Daddy. He always beat me."

(This last statement was apparently disputed by Mrs. Tanaka.)

"Here he did. . . . I'm not staying with him. . . . I'm not staying with him. . . . Is he going to be at the airport? If he's at the airport, I'm not speaking with him. If he's at the airport, I'm not coming. . . . Call me when you talk to him."

Gregory appeared to be moderately agitated by his mother's comments and replies. He seemed taken aback by his mother's failure to provide the kind of reassurances he had received from Mukaro the day before. Toward the end of this exchange with his mother, the apparent reason for Gregory's decision to return, which he had avoided telling me earlier, was revealed.

"The social worker told me [Father] was in jail," Gregory blurted.

My heart sank. Was Gregory's decision to leave based entirely on a possible fabrication by Mukaro? If so, the jig was up. Any notion that Gregory may have had about his father's being safely away in prison was crumbled by his mother's almost cryptic references to Mr. Tanaka's status and whereabouts. Would Gregory interpret this as a betrayal by Mukaro? Certainly, no feeling of trust could survive such a betrayal or perception of betrayal.

These questions that I was conjuring up in my mind would soon be answered. Isaac Mukaro would arrive soon to participate in the meeting that had been planned on Friday involving Dr. Heacock, the State Department psychiatrists from Washington, and myself. I feared the worst: a confrontation between Gregory and Mukaro and a reversal of Gregory's decision to return.

25. The Decision to Return

A T THE END of the February 22 therapy session with Gregory, I received word that the State Department psychiatrists had arrived and were waiting in our third-floor office to meet with us. Gregory remained upstairs while I went down first to see them.

Dr. Steven Pieczenik and Dr. Elmore Rigamer were speaking with Gary Kipling and Tom Ring, who completed the introductions. I briefed them on the latest developments, including what had just transpired in the therapy session. Although all were pleased about Gregory's announced readiness to leave, I voiced my concern that Gregory had been misled about his father's status, and that he might lose trust in Mukaro. Following our brief discussion, the psychiatrists met with Gregory for a while, and then all of us, except Gregory, convened in the conference room. By then Dr. Heacock had arrived and joined us, but Isaac Mukaro still had not arrived.

Dr. Pieczenik immediately assumed the lead role in the meeting. He was no stranger to high-profile and politically explosive situations, having been involved as consultant in numerous hostage negotiations, including those in Iran and Lebanon. He took a direct, no-nonsense approach in outlining the agenda for the meeting:

1. Determine whether Gregory is ready to return to Zimbabwe.
2. Begin preliminary planning for the return.
3. Identify support services that must be in place in Zimbabwe.
4. Consider how the media should be handled.

Item four was of particular concern to Dr. Pieczenik. He felt that extensive—in fact, *any*—media coverage might hamper or sabotage a planned departure. He wanted reassurances and safeguards against any media involvement.

Dr. Heacock and I were supportive of Gregory's departing in the near future. Dr. Heacock observed that "Gregory's ego strengths are in place . . . he readily reconstitutes . . . and uses coping skills effectively." He urged that there be no contact between Gregory and his father for a while, but that his relationship with his mother should be focused upon instead.

I summarized my findings and recommendations, which were discussed in detail in an eleven-page psychological therapy progress summary, copies of which were distributed to all present. Actually, my secretary, Sylvia Norman, was hurriedly typing and photocopying the report as I was presenting my findings verbally; she completed everything just in time for distribution at an opportune moment. The report included my treatment goals, the course of treatment, changes in family constellation and time structuring, changes in presenting symptoms (including progress toward treatment goals), cognitive functioning, revised diagnosis, and recommendations. It was as thorough and comprehensive a therapy summary report as I had ever prepared in my professional career, and it was received extremely well by Drs. Pieczenik and Rigamer. It cited substantial progress toward each of the treatment goals, including the attainment of a new perspective by Gregory about his parents. I qualified my revised diagnoses of Post Traumatic Stress Disorder and Oppositional Disorder by adding the words "Condition improved" after each. I closed the progress section with: "He's feeling more and more like any other normal child, but in all probability he will require much additional work in the area of peer socialization."

My recommendations included continuing Gregory's contacts with his mother, who should be guided in preferable approaches to take; the enrollment of both parents in a parent training program addressing issues of discipline, the understanding of children's misbehavior, family problem-solving, and factors contributing to child abuse; the further development of a trusting relationship with a

Zimbabwean professional (Isaac Mukaro) to serve as a transitional object between New York and Zimbabwe, where he could be relied upon as a dependable, potent resource for Gregory; the continuation of individual psychotherapy for Gregory, with emphasis on redefining changing and conflictual feelings toward each family member, and strengthening adaptive coping skills when dealing with authority. In closing, I emphasized the need for greater predictability for Gregory in the immediate future.

> Gregory would benefit from having a clear understanding of what he might expect from his parents' present living arrangements, his level of contact with each family member, his accessibility to the Zimbabwean professional he meets in New York, and any other factors that might promote his sense of predictability and personal safety.

This extensive list of recommendations constituted my professional definition of the "therapeutic transfer," which had been the subject of such controversy in Judge Weinstein's court on the fourth of January.

After a break for lunch Isaac Mukaro and Bob McMahon arrived, and the meeting was resumed.

Mukaro spoke in soft tones, necessitating extra-attentive efforts on the part of his listeners. He began by acknowledging that reuniting Gregory with his family now would be premature. He detailed the chain of events that would likely occur upon Gregory's return. He explained that, in his position with the Social Welfare Ministry, he could and would immediately petition the courts for a fourteen-day Order of Protection prohibiting Mr. Tanaka from going near Gregory. Such legal action, he explained, could not be initiated until Gregory was present and a participant in the proceedings. This clarified the matter of Mr. Tanaka's status, which had been unclear to that point. Zimbabwean law required the presence and involvement of the child in the pursuit of legal sanctions against the alleged abuser. I raised the point that Gregory was particularly fearful of having a confrontation with his father at the airport.

"Can you get assurances that Mr. Tanaka will not be at the airport?" I asked.

Mukaro responded in a diplomatic fashion, assuring that every effort would be made, but said that he could not guarantee that Mr. Tanaka would not be there. "There's no legal means of keeping him away from the airport," he stressed.

I was disappointed with what he said.

Mukaro continued. He stated that Gregory would reside with the Mukaro family for a short period. Mukaro would then petition the court to order that Gregory be placed in the custody of the Social Welfare Ministry for a period of up to three years. Mukaro's own recommendations would bear heavily on the court's disposition of such a petition. The process, indeed, was quite similar to the one followed in the New York City foster care system. Our only moment of caution came when Mukaro pulled from his briefcase an extremely yellowed copy of the Zimbabwean child-protection laws. It was dated 1922, harking back to British-ruled Rhodesia, which was governed under English law. Mukaro stressed that "the interests of the child must be paramount."

I hesitated to interrupt the very positive feeling shared by all around the conference table, but it was time to confront Mukaro about the false statement attributed to him by Gregory. I turned to him and prefaced my remarks by saying that "there might be a problem."

"Gregory," I continued, "is under the impression that his father is in jail. That seemed to be an important reason for his feeling safe about going back to Zimbabwe. He said that you told him this yesterday, but he received contradictory messages about his father's status when speaking with his mother on the phone this morning."

There was a stony silence for several seconds that seemed like hours. Without flinching, Mukaro clarified his impression of what had transpired between Gregory and him, acknowledging only that he had mentioned to Gregory the possibility of Mr. Tanaka's imprisonment. It was agreed that the misunderstanding had to be straightened out so as to immediately restore any diminished trust on Gregory's part. The meeting broke up, and Mukaro accompanied me to my office, where Gregory and Stephanie Rothstein had been waiting.

Gregory didn't pull any punches. The second we stepped

through the doorway he exclaimed to Mukaro, "You lied to me. You told me that my father was in jail."

Although Gregory was assertive in making the allegation, he was neither excessively angry nor belligerent. Mukaro attempted to clarify what he had said the day before, but he wasn't quite getting the message across.

"Gregory," I interjected, "Isaac told me what the situation was. Do you want me to explain what Isaac said?"

"Yes, but not here. I want to talk with you alone," he proclaimed.

"Where would you like to talk?"

"In the bathroom," declared Gregory.

So now, after two months of nonstop intrigue and drama involving scores of people, including heads of state on two continents, the decision that would bring this ordeal to an end would hinge on an impromptu meeting in a bathroom.

When we entered, Gregory asked, "What did Isaac really say?"

I explained that Isaac had referred only to the possibility of Gregory's father going to jail, but that it must have sounded to Gregory as if his father were already in jail. Perhaps Gregory had heard what he wanted to hear, or perhaps he had actually been misled by Mukaro. I found myself feeling confused and somewhat skeptical, but I proceeded as though I were fully convinced of Mukaro's honesty and integrity.

Our bathroom meeting was brief. We returned to Mukaro and Stephanie. He took the initiative and apologized for any misunderstandings that his remarks of Sunday may have caused. Gregory remained silent.

I asked if Gregory was prepared to forgive Isaac the way he once forgave me in the controversy over the bet.

After a few seconds, Gregory uttered, "I forgive you."

The crisis had passed.

Whereas it had taken Gregory three days to forgive me, he was now much more open to forgiving Mukaro. Ultimately, he would need to call upon such a capacity to forgive if he were ever to resolve his strained relationships with his mother, sisters, and perhaps even his father.

The next day, February 23, Dr. Pieczenik, Dr. Rigamer, and Isaac Mukaro returned to spend more time with Gregory. I went about other business without much involvement with them; I intended to leave early to celebrate my son Jimmy's birthday. The thought that Mukaro had been less than one hundred percent forthright about the imprisonment issue still nagged at me. Everything else about him seemed so honest and engendering of trust. I just needed some additional proof of his honest intentions in order to rest assured that I was not an accomplice to duping Gregory.

The opportunity for verification came when Mukaro asked if he could use my office to prepare an interim report to his supervisors in the Social Welfare Ministry. I consented and asked if he would like to have my secretary type the report for him. He was grateful for the offer, but stipulated that no copies be made, since this was of a highly confidential and sensitive nature. Nevertheless, I was able to sneak a look at the finished report before it was returned to Mukaro.

After glancing over Mukaro's report, I felt much better about things. I was particularly heartened by statements to the effect that "the father will not be in a position to arbitrarily take over without the consent of the Department of Social Welfare, whose main interest in this case is the best interest and welfare of the minor Gregory." Mukaro referred to the likelihood that both parents, particularly the father, "will undergo parent training sessions on issues related to discipline, reinforcement of positive behavior, parent-child communication, and general family problem-solving."

I felt proud that the copy of my report, which I had given to Mukaro the day before, had apparently influenced his thinking in formulating his own recommendations. The cycle was now complete. The interventions and precautions for which we had been arguing painstakingly since December had been espoused first by SSC, then accepted by the courts, then by the public with important assistance from the media, then by members of Congress, then by the State Department, and now finally by an official of the Zimbabwean government.

On Wednesday, February 24, Dr. Pieczenik called from Washington.

"Good news! It looks good for a target date of Sunday night," he announced.

He told me that he had met with Secretary of State George Schultz that morning, just prior to Schultz's departure for the Middle East, and had referred to my report as the basis for a recommendation to move Gregory at this time. Secretary Schultz apparently had been prepared to hold out further and keep Gregory in America indefinitely if his health and welfare so dictated. By Pieczenik's account, Schultz was not going to allow matters of diplomacy to jeopardize a child's well-being. This sounded much more like the Norman Rockwell America in which I grew up, where officials of the government stood for high moral principles, including the basic human rights of all people. "Maybe there is still some hope, after all," I thought.

Dr. Pieczenik thanked me for my professional assistance, but added that he had one major request to make. He asked if Bob McMahon and I would be available to travel to Washington on Friday to meet with some senators who had taken an interest in Gregory's case. The State Department hoped to enlist our assistance in giving the senators our endorsement of the recommendation to send Gregory back to Zimbabwe. Wouldn't that be ironic?

Thursday, February 25, marked the fifteenth and final therapy session that I had with Gregory. I probed to see if he had any second thoughts or reservations about leaving. For the record, I asked if he would give his feelings about leaving on videotape, and he consented.

In answer to a question about his resolve to leave, Gregory said that he was "very sure" about the move. He said he was looking forward to seeing his friend Jeffrey, but he didn't respond to a question about what he would miss most about New York. I tried to ease our separation by expressing my sincere admiration for him and saying that I would miss him. This embarrassed Gregory, who then wanted to curtail our conversation and go from office to office interviewing St. Christopher-Ottilie staff. Before we finished, however, I asked him what I should say if reporters asked me about him in the future.

"Tell them anything they want to know," he said. "Tell them my whole story."

With that, he took the camcorder and started to look for subjects to interview as he slipped into the fantasy role of Gregory O'Brien and, alternately, Bob O'Gregory.

26. On the Hill for the Final Showdown

F ROM THE TIME of the first ruling in Queens family court on December 22, 1987, the U.S. Department of State had maintained continuous *legal* custody of Gregory Tanaka. On a number of occasions, the department had been extremely close to securing *physical* custody, only to be stymied by temporary stays or court rulings. Since mid-January, it had voluntarily refrained from taking physical custody because of public sentiment abetted by the media. Ultimately, I believe, the State Department had refrained from taking any action because of its own revised sense of propriety and the moral imperative to protect the welfare of the child.

Now, on February 26, there was one last party to be heard from before the State Department could finally proceed to assume temporary physical custody of Gregory. Representatives of Congress had to be consulted.

If the State Department had acted without consulting with Congress, no laws would have been broken, but it would have been a politically irresponsible thing to do. State Department officials knew that there were congressmen and senators who had demonstratively supported Gregory's legal fight for asylum in early January. They would not automatically or easily accept the State Department's word that everything was now okay or that Gregory wanted to return to Zimbabwe. Even if it could be shown that Gregory wanted to return, there would still be considerable skepticism over the readiness and willingness of Zimbabwe's child protection system and the government of Zimbabwe to carry out promises to protect Gregory.

There were major risks to proceeding without congressional blessings. Disaffected senators or congressmen could delay Gregory's departure by seeking injunctive relief, perhaps through citing some remote law that no one had thought of yet. Alternatively, a bill or bills could be introduced pertaining to Gregory in particular or to human rights violations or diplomatic immunity of minors in general. Determined congressional figures could, at least, cause another protracted public struggle. If there is one thing that provokes the people on the Hill, it's the failure of the executive branch to consult and collaborate with Congress, particularly in foreign affairs.

For some senators, Gregory's case was as much an issue of American foreign policy as it was a question of a child's safety and rights. Some were highly critical of the Reagan administration's policy—or lack of policy—on the nations of Africa. Differences of opinion existed concerning where America should stand vis-à-vis the emerging independent African countries, some of which were far to the left in their philosophies. Strong feelings were raised about the license to flaunt and break American laws that many foreign diplomats seem to believe is inherent in the conventions of diplomatic immunity. The case of Gregory Tanaka could thus be used to illustrate flaws in Reagan administration policy by members of Congress who wished to exploit the case politically.

Therefore the State Department turned to St. Christopher-Ottilie to help them convince members of Congress that returning Gregory to Zimbabwe was now in his best interest. Bob McMahon and I were asked to fly to Washington Thursday evening so that we would be available to attend an early morning briefing at the State Department on Friday.

As we were finishing breakfast on Friday morning, we were met at the hotel restaurant by a very personable man, Shaw Smith. As he ushered us through the State Department building's entrance on C Street, the trappings of history and power that surrounded us didn't fail to register with me. I had "goose bumps."

We were escorted to the office of Undersecretary of State Richard Williamson, one of several undersecretaries who would participate in the morning's activities. Williamson's office was quite large and impressive, decorated throughout with Teddy Roosevelt memorabilia. He detailed the agenda for the morning, which included a preliminary briefing in the adjacent conference room.

Seated around the conference table were Dr. Pieczenik, Dr. Heacock, Bob McMahon, myself, Richard Williamson, Shaw Smith, and five or six other State Department officials.

The purpose of the briefing was to establish a game plan to prepare everyone for the Capitol Hill meeting to follow. It felt funny, if not awkward, to be included in a State Department strategy session after two months of considering myself on the opposing side. What astounded me most was the level of concern and apprehension in the air regarding the upcoming meeting. Until then I hadn't fully appreciated how important it was for the State Department to receive congressional support in this case. Implicit was the message that Gregory might not be sent if agreement was not reached.

A question was addressed to me by one of the State Department people: "What will you tell them if they ask why it's so important for the child to leave now?"

Before I had a chance to answer, another State Department official, who was not, to my knowledge, a mental health expert, took the liberty of posing a possible response: "If we don't send him now, there will be a regression. He'll regress. That's what you should tell them," he said.

"Regression, yeah, I like that," offered another State Department person.

I was peeved—if not insulted—by what was going on. But I tried not to show my displeasure.

"I think, gentlemen," I interjected, "that I would not feel comfortable with saying that. A more accurate assessment of what I think would happen is that Gregory's development might be arrested if he is prevented from proceeding with resolving important conflictual issues. His growth may be hindered if his energies are all tied up with a family situation in limbo."

"We don't want you to say anything that you're not comfortable with," offered Dr. Pieczenik, and the tension lifted somewhat.

I informed the group that I had brought a videotape of my last session with Gregory, which had taken place the day before. If there were any congressional questions about Gregory's resolve to leave, they could be dispelled by viewing the segment of the tape addressing his departure.

We took a long walk to an area where ex-hostages are debriefed and where video equipment is available. After viewing about ten minutes of the tape, we headed out to the Capitol.

The 10:30 A.M. meeting was in the Senate Foreign Relations Committee Room, a room of considerable size and grandeur. Light was provided by immense chandeliers that descended over the largest conference table I had ever seen.

The contingent from the State Department, including Bob and myself, greeted the congressional figures who were awaiting us. Senator Claiborne Pell, the chairman of the U.S. Senate Committee on Foreign Relations, and his assistant welcomed us warmly. We were introduced to Paul Stockton, an assistant to Senator Daniel Moynihan of New York, and Paul Christianson, an assistant to Senator Jesse Helms of North Carolina. Senators Moynihan and Helms were temporarily tied up in other hearings, and we were told that we could start the meeting without them. I took a seat at the midpoint of the oval table, flanked by Bob to my right and Drs. Heacock and Pieczenik to my left. The other State Department officials were seated to Dr. Pieczenik's left, extending to the end of the table. The congressional people sat across from us, except for Paul Christianson, who sat at the head of the table.

Senator Pell began by clarifying that his role was to be a moderator and possibly a mediator in the proceedings. He explained that the case was of particular interest to Senators Moynihan and Helms, both of whom had requested the meeting. He noted that in their absence both senators had asked that their assistants stand in for them.

With that, Paul Christianson took the floor. Addressing the State Department officials, he aggressively challenged them on how they could be so sure that Gregory would be protected once back in Zimbabwe.

"How do you know that they won't just turn him right back over to his father as soon as he gets off the plane?" asked Christianson.

"We've got iron–clad reassurances that Zimbabwe's child protection laws will be enforced" was the State Department response.

"But how can you believe them? Do you have their reassurances in writing?" Christianson asked.

With each exchange, the atmosphere heated up. Christianson seemed genuinely perturbed that the State Department was so ready to send Gregory back to a risky situation. With each charge from Christianson came a State Department rebuttal. After fifteen minutes of this there was no change in anyone's position. If anything, Christianson showed even greater resolve against any decision to move Gregory. The conversation was getting nowhere, when the two large doors behind me opened. All eyes turned to the doors as Senator Helms, the senior Republican senator from North Carolina, walked in.

Jesse Helms, a senator since 1973, was one of the most powerful and influential men in all of Congress. He had a reputation for being a staunch conservative with very definite ideas about some key moral issues of the time, including abortion, busing for integration, and school prayer. He was vehemently against the first two and for the latter. Most of all, Senator Helms was known throughout Washington for his keen interest in children. It was Senator Helms who, at the height of the legal battle in early January, announced that he was prepared to introduce legislation that would have made Gregory an American citizen. The senator, frequently intimidating to others, bowed to no one. His readiness to stand up for his convictions regardless of political consequence made him one of the most independent forces in the Senate. It was Helms, rather than Senator Moynihan, who most concerned the people from the State Department. Senator Moynihan was likely to support moving Gregory if St. Christopher-Ottilie was in favor of it. This would be consistent with his steadfast support of our efforts since the first week of January. Senator Helms, however, was not nearly as likely to go along with any recommendation that was contrary to his perception of the right path for the child.

"Good morning, Senator," several people at the table uttered. Jesse Helms nodded and ambled slowly, ever so slowly, toward the other side of the table. His presence commanded everyone's attention, such was his stature. All discussion ceased.

There was silence for a few moments, then Helms asked in his distinct southern accent, "You're not going to send the boy back, are you?"

There was no reply from anyone.

Senator Helms had established his advantage before he had even reached his chair, which happened to be at the midpoint of the conference table, facing the door and directly across from where I was sitting.

"Give me one good reason why we should send the boy away. He's safe here," Senator Helms exclaimed.

"Senator, he's ready to go. The boy wants to go back home," said Dr. Pieczenik.

"C'mon, you don't think he'll ever be able to live back there, do you?" the senator retorted. "I think he should stay here. If there's one thing I can't stand it's people who would do that to a child."

One by one, the State Department people took a crack at reversing the senator's opinion. He didn't accept their statement. He was not the type of person who would take someone else's word on faith alone. He needed more proof, more substantiation than they were offering. Bob and I sat quietly as this fascinating exchange occurred. Finally, I thought it time to introduce myself.

"Senator, my name is Dr. Leonard Gries. I'm a psychologist who has been treating Gregory for the past two months. Until recently, these people to my left were adversaries of mine. I opposed their efforts at taking Gregory by force and sending him to Zimbabwe prematurely. As his therapist, I've always had Gregory's needs uppermost in my mind."

I was encouraged by the fact that the senator was eyeing me intently. He seemed interested in hearing what I had to say.

"From your remarks before," I continued, "it sounds like we

are considering not just whether Gregory should leave now, but whether he will ever leave—whether we should make Gregory an American for life."

"And what's wrong with that?" the senator bellowed.

"Because he has a dream, a hope that someday, in some way, he might be able to get closer to his family."

I explained this statement by first recalling Gregory's condition when he came into foster care.

"When I met Gregory for the first time, he was a terrified little boy who wanted to have nothing to do with either of his parents. He was extremely angry with them for the harsh treatment he had received. He also suffered from a disorder similar to that found in many veterans of combat: Post-Traumatic Stress Disorder. With such disorder, the child was prone to brief psychotic-like episodes in which he believed that he was again in danger, even when no danger was present. He could not trust anyone, particularly not anyone from Zimbabwe. He felt terribly vulnerable and out of control. In his attempts to gain a sense of control, he typically opposed and challenged authority figures, thereby antagonizing them into acting more oppressively toward him. This only substantiated his feelings of being alienated and victimized.

"Things have changed since then. Now Gregory is able to trust. He no longer yearns for revenge, although he is still quite fearful of his father. Significantly, he has come to see his mother in a different light. Instead of viewing her as a disinterested accomplice to her husband, Gregory now sees her as a victim, too. The bond with his mother has come back into focus for Gregory, as have his feelings of love for her. He has moved in the direction of wanting to repair his disrupted relationship with her, and he cannot do that while she's there and he is here."

As I caught my breath, Bob slipped me a note that read, "Keep going, you're on a roll." With that encouragement, I proceeded.

"As for Gregory's father, no one can condone what he did. We can think of him as being a 'low life' who should be sent away for a long time and severely punished. But that wouldn't solve that troubled family's situation. As difficult as it is to believe, there are abusive parents who have been treated and trained to discontinue their abuse. When Gregory heard about that, it gave him an ever so slight a glimmer of hope that change in his father is possible. Dare we take that hope away from him? The only way in which Gregory can pursue his dream of family reconciliation is if he lives closer to home. That is his main interest. The alternative is for him to spend the remainder of his childhood here, in perpetual limbo, never really knowing what his permanent status will be. No one knows whether any type of family reconciliation will ever be feasible. But before Gregory ever lets go of the dream, he has to make an attempt and see for himself. If he remained here as a candidate for adoption, the outlook for a successful adoption would be bleak as long as Gregory still clung to his dream. It must be resolved one way or the other."

Senator Helms listened quietly and attentively throughout my six- or seven-minute presentation. For the first few moments after I finished, he gave no indication of how he felt about what I had said. I was impressed by the way he had allowed me to proceed without interrupting or challenging me along the way. He really seemed intent on listening to me and processing what I had to say, without rigidly clinging to any preconceived biases.

Finally, he spoke. "You make a very convincing argument. Your points are well taken."

At that point, Bob chimed in, explaining his role as executive director of St. Christopher-Ottilie and Gregory's guardian *ad litem*.

"Senator, I've been in the child welfare field for a quarter of a century. I was appointed guardian *ad litem* by Judge Weinstein, and I have the child's best interests uppermost in my mind. I would not be here recommending Gregory's transfer unless I sincerely believed that this is the right thing for him."

Turning to his aide, Senator Helms said, "I've heard enough." He instructed his aide to "keep on asking whatever questions you want, and let me know about it later."

With that, the senator stood up, smiled, shook hands with everyone, and left.

The meeting resumed, but I knew that we had already succeeded. By first establishing my position as independent of the State Department, then reviewing Gregory's progress to date and emphasizing the need for giving Gregory the opportunity to repair his estranged relationship with family members, I was able to simultaneously reach Senator Helms on an emotional, intellectual, and pragmatic level. Once the senator had left, Christianson half-heartedly pursued some remaining concerns, but without the verve and determination observed earlier.

He asked why it was so important for Gregory to leave on Sunday. "Why couldn't it wait until later in the week, when written reassurances from Zimbabwe could be secured?" he asked.

"There are two main reasons, Mr. Christianson," I replied. "As an abused child, Gregory's life has been long out of his control. He never knew when his safety or even his life would be in jeopardy. For such a child, asserting control over his own destiny is an extremely important psychological need. We can help give Gregory that feeling of control by complying with his request to leave on Sunday with Mr. Mukaro. For us to ignore his request would be to suggest that he has as little say in his life as before.

"The second reason pertains to Zimbabwe's probable reaction to our demands for written verification of its plans to protect Gregory. I was impressed by the strong need for Zimbabwe to demonstrate its sovereignty to the world. We would interfere with that objective if we in America forced them into giving us written assurances. Even if we succeeded in pressuring them into giving a guarantee, would it be worth more than the paper it was written on? If we don't trust their word when they say they'll protect Gregory, then why should we trust them to adhere to the terms of a written agreement?"

How ironic, I thought. The issue of trust just kept permeating this case from beginning to end. Could Gregory trust his family? If not, could he trust other Zimbabweans? If not, could he trust me or Gary? Could we at St. Christopher-Ottilie trust the State Department? Could the State Department trust us? Could the federal judges and Supreme Court justices trust the State Department? Could we trust the media? Could Gregory finally trust Isaac Mukaro? Could *we* trust Isaac?

The answer to all of the above questions could be answered in the same way: yes, in due time.

Only one issue remained in doubt. Could the Zimbabwean government be trusted at its word? In order to find the answer to that question, the risk of sending Gregory back would have to be taken.

As lunchtime in Washington approached, it was virtually unanimous. The State Department, St. Christopher-Ottilie, members of Congress, and, most important, Gregory all agreed that it was time to take that big risk. By afternoon the decision for Gregory to leave for Zimbabwe on Sunday was finalized.

27. Farewell!

THE QUESTION OF how to say goodbye to a child who had totally consumed our lives for over two months remained, the one last task in this saga.

Bob McMahon and his wife, Kathy, arranged for a small send-off party at their Sea Cliff home on Saturday, February 27. So many people had been involved and had been instrumental in furthering Gregory's cause. So many people cared. It would be nice to give everyone the opportunity to personally wish Gregory good luck, but this might have proven too taxing for Gregory.

It was decided instead to limit the guests to those who had been personally involved with Gregory. Stephanie, Yara, and Zeyda were there. Tom and Gary came, along with Gary's son Jeremy. Bob's secretary, Mary, was there with her husband. Dr. Heacock came, and I came with my wife and family. I asked my brother Phil, who is a professional cinematographer, to take some video so that we could have a permanent record of the farewell.

The atmosphere was very lighthearted and cheerful throughout the afternoon. The other children, who also included Bob's three daughters, occupied Gregory in the basement game room for much of the time. Later, farewell gifts were presented as Kathy brought out a big going-away ice cream cake. Among my gifts to Gregory were the sunglasses from my car, which I had promised him about six weeks earlier.

A little later, when some of the guests had already left, Bob came over and whispered that he had Bob O'Brien on the phone. He had said he would be willing to come over and meet Gregory if Gregory so desired. I took Gregory aside and told him of O'Brien's offer. He was thrilled at the idea of meeting his favorite TV newsman in person. O'Brien arrived after dark, armed with a few gifts, including a Fox-TV microphone logo. Shy at first, Gregory eventually warmed up and slipped into his favorite role of news reporter. That was his way of retaining control—his way of asking questions rather than having to answer them.

But when Bob O'Brien attempted to turn the tables and ask Gregory a few questions about his upcoming trip, Gregory tightened up and became quiet. He did not want to have the fun interrupted by something that still aroused anxiety for him.

I interrupted, saying that I had something to tell Gregory that I had been putting off for over a month, but I felt that this was the right moment. I told him about the many people who had contacted us in January to voice their concerns and lend support to protecting Gregory. People from all walks of life, from all over the United States, had been worried about him and were on his side. This information wasn't totally new to Gregory, who certainly was aware of the media coverage of his story. But then I added something that surprised him.

"Gregory, I didn't tell you this before, but I even received a letter from a bunch of school children in California who were very worried about you."

Gregory, half-smiling, replied, "I don't believe you. No one in California sent any letter."

"I'm not making this up. I really have the letter."

"If it's true, then show me the letter," Gregory demanded.

"I have it at home, but if you want, I'll bring it to the airport tomorrow. They and many more children and adults want to know that you're okay. They want to know about you."

Gregory was deeply flattered and touched. It's one thing to have some interested adults engage in a legal battle over you. It's another thing to have peers three thousand miles away thinking of you and caring about you. For Gregory, a child who never seemed to feel he belonged at school, who felt like an outsider to his family and his peers, this revelation was extremely meaningful. He was overjoyed the next day when I fulfilled my promise and gave him a copy of the letter.

> We, the undersigned students at Calmont School in California, feel we have the right to be informed of the fate of nine-year-old Zimbabwean Gregory Tanaka. We wish to be informed if he remains in the United States, or if he has been returned to his country. If he has been returned to his country, we want to know under whose custody and what has been planned to rectify the frightening abusive environment in his home. What is being done to protect Gregory and his brothers and sisters? We are not voters—but we are future voters. We are U.S. citizens, and though we may be minor in years, we are major in rights.
>
> Respectfully,
> *(Signed by nine fourth-grade*
> *students and their teachers)*

After hearing about the letter from the school children, Gregory felt that he wanted them and others to know about him. He looked at me and said, "Tell them my whole story. Tell them anything they want to know. I want them to know. But you say it; I don't want to say it."

Gregory consented to conversing with Bob O'Brien and me about his return home. Phil caught it on tape, and it was aired two nights later as Gregory made his way back to Zimbabwe.

The party ended much later than anyone had expected. We were all exhausted, but I had difficulty falling asleep that night. I tossed and turned while I mulled over Gregory's directive to "tell them my whole story." What should be said publicly about Gregory and all that he went through? His privacy had been lost long before, when news that a diplomat's son had been brutally tortured had broken into the headlines in mid-December. In early January, I wittingly contributed to further incursions into his privacy in an effort to enlist media and public support to save him. This was uncharacteristic of the confidential professional-client relationship that usually prevails, but it had become a moral necessity.

Now, with Gregory prepared to leave, his partially exposed story could easily be misinterpreted and misconstrued by viewers and readers, who had heard little of him since the Supreme Court decision in January. Many thought that he had been forcibly sent back in January, and most assumed that he was already in the hands of his father. They knew all about the abuse without knowing about its cause and impact on Gregory. They knew much about the way he had been victimized, but knew nothing about other dimensions in his life: his courage, his resourcefulness, and his sense of humor.

A half-truth can be more damaging than no truth, I reasoned. People had been bombarded with bits of facts and information for two weeks and then virtually nothing thereafter. That could lead only to distorted views of Gregory and his family, as well as of child abuse in general. Shouldn't the public be given a complete picture of what child abuse is all about and how it had engulfed Gregory and his family? Shouldn't there be an understanding of the roles played by the various governmental agencies, private agencies, and the courts in the system designed to protect abused and neglected children?

The seeds for writing this book were thus planted as I tossed and turned in bed that Saturday night.

In retrospect, what lessons or observations can be made from the case of Gregory? Freud's method of free association may provide me the most expeditious means for answering such questions:

- Child abuse is a growing problem that cuts across cultural, racial, economic, and class lines.
- The causes of child abuse are manifold, extending from misunderstandings about how to discipline the child, to psychological factors impinging on the abusive parent, to the influences of substance abuse.
- The non-abusing parent is often a frightened victim herself or himself.

- The abused child suffers from devastated self-esteem, a low sense of self-efficacy, and a feeling of total vulnerability and lack of control.
- The abused child reacts either by being overly compliant, by trying to assert control in safer settings, by countering his sense of weakness through acting aggressively, or by being distrustful of almost everyone.
- Over one-half of all abused children suffer from Post-Traumatic Stress Disorder.
- School difficulties and delays in development often result in abuse at home and worsen as a consequence of abuse.
- The psychological results of abuse can be ameliorated through psychotherapeutic intervention.
- The relief and sanctuary provided to the abused child by a foster care placement is a crucial component of the overall treatment plan.
- Intervention in child abuse does not automatically lead to dissolution of the family.
- Even a child with a history of severe and chronic abuse may have and seek to retain strong bonds to either or both parents.
- The child, caught between his love of the parent and fear and/or anger toward the parent exhibits changes in mood and behavior reflective of such conflict.
- Opportunities to resolve the parental love-hate conflict must be given to the abused child; if not, the fantasy of a family reconciliation may plague him for the remainder of his childhood.
- Parent training, individual psychotherapy, marital counseling, and substance abuse counseling are some of the techniques that can be effective in eliminating a parent's abusive behavior.
- Counseling for the entire family is usually required in order to maintain the gains made by the child and his parents.
- Our family court system succeeds in protecting the welfare of numerous child victims and potential victims, but does not protect all.

- Our entire legal system is unable to protect the abused child of a foreign diplomat because of the principle of diplomatic immunity.
- There is no legal provision open to our courts for disregarding international law when it conflicts with the protection of an individual's human rights, as was the case with Gregory.
- When the chips are down, matters of state and politics may be given precedence over matters of individual rights—even in our own United States of America.
- The voice of the people contributes significantly in our checks-and-balances system of government; ultimately, it is the final guarantor of an individual's rights after all administrative and legal venues are exhausted.
- It ain't over 'til it's over.

There was still one more day before we could really say that "it was over." Sunday, February 28, was a brisk, clear, typical winter's day. Gregory awoke at the Kipling home where he had been staying for the last three days. According to Gary, Gregory was a bit jittery as the day progressed.

"Will Isaac really keep his word? Will my father be at the airport? What if they take my wallet with all the addresses of my American friends?"

These were just some of his concerns. Gary answered each question and tried his best to reassure Gregory, who remained apprehensive but not overly fearful. Some of his nervousness was dissipated when Gary took him to buy a traveling outfit, including some shiny new shoes. Finally, in the late afternoon, they drove to the St. Christopher-Ottilie Residential Treatment Facility campus in Queens, where they made their rendezvous with the remainder of the farewell party: Stephanie Rothstein, Steve Pieczenik, Bob Moeller, Isaac Mukaro, and myself.

I asked Gregory to join me alone in one of the offices so we could say goodbye in private, and so I could answer any last-minute questions he might have. He was calmly excited (if I might be excused the contradiction). I gave him a copy of the letter from

California I had promised him on Saturday. I also gave him a small traveling package containing some baseball cards, a miniature jet plane, and a video game. Surely he would need as much diversion as possible to help him survive his long, grueling journey. I reached in my pocket and removed a penny. I referred to it as my lucky penny, suggesting that good things would happen when he carried it. Gregory was pleased to receive any help he could get. Noticing his favorable reaction, I took a one-dollar bill from my wallet and told him he could hold on to this lucky dollar as well.

A few minutes later, as we were about to enter the State Department car for the ride to the airport, Gregory turned to me with a serious expression and asked, "Can I hold on to the lucky penny and spend the lucky dollar?"

Before leaving, I spoke briefly with Dr. Pieczenik. He was to accompany Gregory and Isaac all the way to Zimbabwe. He was hopeful that everything would go smoothly, but he still showed some apprehension of his own. He really didn't know what to expect. Despite all the reassurances, was it even remotely possible that Gregory's father would be at the airport in Harare, waiting to take Gregory back into custody? Would the Zimbabwean government and Isaac Mukaro carry out the protective steps that had been promised?

Leaving nothing to chance, Dr. Pieczenik had secured a photo of Philip Tanaka. He showed it to me. "If I see him at the airport, I'm not getting off the plane with Gregory," he said.

This gave me mixed feelings. I was encouraged by the determination of this State Department psychiatrist to go to whatever extreme necessary to protect Gregory. I was shaken, however, by the thought of everything falling apart if we and Gregory were betrayed by false promises from the Zimbabwean government.

The drive to John F. Kennedy International Airport took about ten minutes. As we turned onto the Belt Parkway from the Van Wyck Expressway, a police escort joined us in front and back. As the lights flashed and the sirens wailed, Gregory softly and expectantly announced, "A half-hour left in America."

The entourage drove right onto the tarmac, where a British

Caledonia 747 was waiting. We got out of the car, but there was nothing much more to say.

I hugged Gregory. "Good luck. Have a safe trip."

In a twinkling, he was ascending the plane and then out of view. Stephanie left to go home, but Gary and I retreated to the VIP lounge of British Caledonia Airlines. In the lounge were some New York City policemen who had been part of the escort, Bob Moeller and his driver, and an official of the Zimbabwean mission to the U.N. In a symbolic way, all the factions had come together for this one final moment. There was an air of relief and laughter as we waited for word that the plane had taken off. An impromptu sports trivia quiz developed.

"Which player hit more home runs than any major leaguer during the decade of the 1950s?" I asked.

Mickey Mantle, Willie Mays, Ralph Kiner, and Ted Williams were some of the answers given.

"It was Duke Snider," I announced with pride. "The best center-fielder of his day." I always loved giving it to Yankee fans.

Suddenly, a voice blared out from one of the officer's walkie-talkies. It was a communication from the squad car on the tarmac behind Gregory's plane.

"The wheels are up," the voice announced to everyone in the lounge. A brief cheer went up.

As we left the lounge, I picked up a complimentary copy of one of the English newspapers. The back page headline of the *Sunday Mail* read in bold, black print: "IT'S OVER!"

Indeed, it was—for me, for St. Christopher-Ottilie, and for the many people involved since mid-December.

It takes a total of thirty-eight and a half hours to travel from New York to Harare. Gregory's plane took off from Kennedy International at 7:45 P.M. on Sunday evening and arrived in London at 7:30 A.M., local time. The three travelers spent most of the day in a London hotel and departed on an Air Zimbabwe plane Monday evening at 8:40 P.M. The flight lasted nine and three-quarters hours until the destination, Lusaka, Zambia, was reached. After a layover of about eight hours, the trio flew the last one-hour leg, arriving in

Harare Tuesday at 5:05 P.M., local time. Gregory handled this extremely long journey in fine fashion. His self-control and cooperation were excellent throughout. As the plane taxied into the terminal at the Harare airport, both Gregory and Dr. Pieczenik grew tense. The plane came to a halt. Dr. Pieczenik asked Mukaro to remain seated with Gregory while he disembarked to assess the situation at the terminal gate. He had to know who was there and what to expect before taking Gregory off the plane.

As he entered the terminal gate, Dr. Pieczenik was greeted by a representative of the Zimbabwean government. As they shook hands, the doctor glimpsed a woman and some young boys nearby. He couldn't be sure, but he thought she must be Leila Tanaka.

With Mrs. Tanaka were three friends of Gregory. Just then, out of the corner of his eye, Dr. Pieczenik spotted a familiar face. He took a closer look at the man standing about fifteen yards from him. His heart sank. It was Philip Tanaka.

Dr. Pieczenik acted quickly. He went back to the Zimbabwean official and informed him that he would not let Gregory off the plane while Mr. Tanaka was there. The official excused himself and made a call to his superior.

Dr. Pieczenik returned to the plane, where Gregory guessed correctly the reason for the delay. Minutes passed, then hours.

Two and a half hours later the coast was clear. Philip Tanaka was gone. He had acquiesced to pressure brought on him through the intercession of none other than Robert Mugabe, president of Zimbabwe. The final link in the chain of trust was now complete. The Zimbabwean government was now committed to the same noble goal that we had been pursuing since December: the protection of the health and welfare of a young child.

Epilogue

GREGORY TANAKA lived with Isaac Mukaro's family for three days after arriving in Zimbabwe. As promised, Mukaro petitioned for and received a restraining order preventing Philip Tanaka from contacting or going near Gregory except during supervised visits to be arranged when Gregory was deemed ready. The courts placed Gregory under the legal protective custody of the Department of Social Welfare for a period of up to three years. The parents of Gregory's close friend, Jeffrey, were designated by the courts to be Gregory's surrogate parents.

On Friday, March 4, 1988, Gregory was placed in a residential boarding school outside Harare. Regular visits with his mother and sisters were immediately scheduled. Ironically, this was the same kind of boarding school to which the Tanakas had contemplated sending Gregory several years earlier, when, prior to his father's assignment to the Zimbabwean mission to the U.N., he had first experienced difficulties in school.

One month later, on April 3, the *New York Times* reported Gregory's status: "He is in a foster home in Harare. . . . He has regularly planned visits with his mother." Gregory's father was reported to be "undergoing counseling under the auspices of the Social Welfare Ministry and his church."

About a week before the *New York Times* article appeared, Gary and I each sent brief notes to Gregory in care of Isaac Mukaro. The notes said that all of us were still thinking of Gregory and wishing him well. With my note I included several snapshots from the farewell party. We invited Gregory to reply, but weeks, then months passed without any answer. There were growing doubts whether he ever even received either note.

As summer 1988 slipped into fall, curiosity about Gregory's fate grew. Anyone who knew of our involvement with the case inevitably posed the question, "Whatever became of that boy from Africa?"

More specific questions were:

"Where is he living?"

"Is he seeing his mother?"

"Is there any contact between Gregory and his father?"

"Is Gregory still frightened of his father?"

"Where is he attending school, and how is he?"

"Is Gregory still receiving therapy?"

"Are either of his parents involved in counseling?"

"Is family therapy occurring or contemplated?"

"Is Gregory in any danger of further abuse?"

"Is he happy?"

It had been hoped that at least some of the answers to these questions would come as a result of follow-up contacts between the State Department and the Zimbabwean government. If any such contacts were made, they were made without any of us at St. Christopher-Ottilie being informed. In the absence of any information, my own apprehension and concern for Gregory's welfare grew. Doubt about the wisdom of supporting his return to Zimbabwe began to surface.

What if they had simply returned him to his father? I thought. Is it possible that we had sent Gregory back for more of the same physical abuse?

I felt a moral obligation to ascertain Gregory's fate, but how to accomplish this task posed still another challenge. The State Department could be contacted, but would ultimately be limited to whatever information the Zimbabwean government chose to release. If bad news was involved, would either government risk rekindling the political sensitivities that had apparently been put to rest at the end of February? There had to be a way to get accurate follow-up information about Gregory. Christmas was approaching as the one-year anniversary of Gregory's placement with St. Christopher-Ottilie arrived. Finally, I thought of the most obvious approach. I had to speak to Gregory's parents myself.

On Sunday, December 18, I placed a call to the same phone number that Gregory had used in late February to reach his mother. It was never actually clear just whose phone number it was, but I assumed that the number belonged to a friend or relative of Mrs. Tanaka.

An adult male answered the phone. I asked to speak with Mrs. Tanaka, and he replied that she was out of the country. I introduced myself and explained that I was calling to inquire about Gregory and to wish him a Merry Christmas. It was a full ten minutes before I realized that the Mrs. Tanaka he referred to as being out of the country was not Gregory's mother, but her cousin. The man gave me the phone number of Philip and Leila Tanaka, and suggested that I call them.

"If you call them now, you may be able to speak to Gregory," he said. "He just came home for the holidays."

This was my invitation to question the man about Gregory's status, and as much of a history as I could get.

"Gregory is in a boarding school. He comes home to his parents on weekends and holidays."

"Oh, I didn't know that Gregory stayed with his parents," I exclaimed. "How is he doing with his father?"

"At first he was afraid to see his parents, but after they saw each other they talked. They really got along."

On completing this conversation, I phoned the Tanaka residence. After two rings, a faint, familiar voice said, "Hello." It was Gregory.

Gregory sounded calm and subdued throughout our ten-minute conversation. He generally answered my questions in a yes-no fashion, without offering much in the way of spontaneous talk. He confirmed that he'd been spending weekends at home with his parents while going to a boarding school during the week. He said that he was feeling fine, having a good time at school, and that he was happy. When asked about the lucky penny that I had given him, Gregory said that he still had it and that it provided him with luck "sometimes."

I asked him whether he had made up with his father, but his reply was inaudible. I refrained from pursuing what may have still been a very sensitive area for Gregory. If he still was having difficulties with his father, it certainly would not have been possible for Gregory to discuss them while other family members were nearby. In closing, Gregory asked me to give his address to Jeremy Kipling so that they might exchange letters. I wished him a Merry Christmas and asked to speak with his mother.

Mrs. Tanaka was very friendly and spontaneous during our conversation. After asking about the weather in New York, she answered several of my questions pertaining to Gregory.

"Have things been patched up between Gregory and his father?"

"Oh yes!"

"There are no ill effects from what happened last year?" I continued.

She giggled and answered, "No."

"How is Gregory doing in school?"

"Oh, he's doing well . . . he's happy."

When I expressed my interest in someday visiting Zimbabwe and making a personal call, Mrs. Tanaka said, "Oh that would be nice. When do you intend to come?"

Finally, she thanked me for calling and wished me a Merry Christmas. Mrs. Tanaka's openness and lack of defensiveness was in marked contrast to what I had observed eleven months earlier. If she had anything to hide, it was certainly not apparent from her demeanor.

This friendly Christmas call answered some very important questions, and raised others. Most important, Gregory was okay. He sounded cautious, but he was not in crisis. He was once again a part of the Tanaka family. He was still "in one piece," thereby confirming the fact that the therapeutic transfer had achieved its aim.

But what about Gregory's life at school and at home? Was he really doing well at school, or was he still having difficulties with authority and academics? Was physical punishment relied upon at home? Was Gregory once again being subjected to physical abuse? The phone call could not answer these questions.

Some questions may remain unanswered for the remainder of Gregory's childhood—or forever. A certain degree of uncertainty will remain with all of us involved in the case. This is one of the unfortunate "givens" of foster care. Professionals work diligently at restoring emotional balance to children in care and at guiding natural parents through rehabilitative efforts, while simultaneously attempting to reunite the family. Sometimes the prognosis for family reunification is very obvious, but often the true readiness of all parties involved remains somewhat in doubt.

Once a child is discharged back to his or her natural parents, a three- to six-month follow-up is usually conducted by a caseworker to ensure adherence to discharge plans and to monitor whether the discharge is actually working. Monitoring may take the form of a once-per-month home visit by the caseworker, and before you know it, the child and his or her family are once again on their own. Then uncertainty may linger in the minds of those who worked on the case. Did the once-alcoholic mother revert to drinking? Did the once-physically abusive father resume the beatings? Did the once-neglectful parents return to their irresponsible ways? Will the child find his way back into the foster care system?

Unfortunately, recidivism is an all-too-frequent occurrence. Social service workers who know this may grow cynical and skeptical about their own efforts at permanently changing the lives of children and families. Is it all worth it? The answer is, of course, it's worth it! We may not be capable of totally removing uncertainty and risk from the lives of Gregory or other clients, but our efforts can and do provide hope. They give a child and a parent a second or third chance to realize a dream that spans cultures, countries, and generations. It is the dream of belonging to, being loved by, and achieving an enduring, positive identity through one's family.